TIGER VIRTUES

18 PROVEN PRINCIPLES FOR WINNING AT GOLF AND IN LIFE

BY ALEX TRESNIOWSKI

RUNNING PRESS
PHILADELPHIA • LONDON

9   8   7   6   5   4   3   2   1
Digit on the right indicates the number of this printing

Library of Congress Control Number: 2004097155

ISBN 0-7624-2338-2

Cover design by Whitney Cookman
Interior design by Dustin Summers
Edited by Greg Jones
Typography: Bembo, Copperplate, Goudy

This book may be ordered by mail from the publisher.
Please include $2.50 for postage and handling.
But try your bookstore first!

Running Press Book Publishers
125 South Twenty-second Street
Philadelphia, Pennsylvania 19103-4399

Visit us on the web!
www.runningpress.com

To Catherine Jantz
Tiger's No. 1 Fan

CONTENTS

FOREWORD

by Dr. Jim Loehr
Author of *The Power of Full Engagement*

Sport is something we care a lot about but doesn't really matter in the big picture of life. And golf is no exception. It's hard to imagine how different our lives would be were we to suddenly discover that our ultimate purpose in life was to get a little round ball to drop into a cup in the fewest number of tries. We all breathe a sigh of relief that this is not our ultimate reason for living. Most would agree that what really matters in life is character, integrity, kindness, strength, resiliency, ethics, hope and compassion for others. Most would also agree that surgeons matter, so do air traffic controllers, nuclear power plant operators, law enforcement officers, care givers, soldiers and the list goes on. From the ranks of these come our real heroes. The link between competitive sport and genuine heroism or virtue, however, seems like a stretch indeed. So, that brings us to the significance of this book.

Most of my professional life, more than three decades, I have been on a mission to answer a single question, a question I believe deeply matters to most everyone. Put simply, the question is this: What is the pathway we must follow as human beings to go from ordinary to extraordinary in the most import areas of our lives? Passion, laser focus, confidence, vision and mental clarity are part of that pathway for sure. So are virtues like humility, honesty, perspective, hope, zest for life, and integrity. And this is precisely where the life of a golfer by the name of Tiger Woods starts to matter. Tiger's greatness is unsurpassed in the history of golf. He has in fact reset the boundaries of how the game is played. He has redefined what's possible and, in the process, chartered a path to extraordinary that leaves us awestruck.

Not unlike my own mission, Alex Tresniowski has been on a mission to illuminate the pathway Tiger Woods, his parents and his coaches forged to gain access to the world of the extraordinary. "Tiger's Virtues" represents the culmination of that mission. Alex brilliantly brings to light Tiger's meticulous preparation, his fierce resolve, his passion for excellence, his rage for perfection and his total commitment to his training. He also brilliantly illuminates the profound impact special people had on Tiger's remarkable development both personally and professionally. Perhaps most intriguing, however, is how the book explores the role virtue has played in Tiger's extraordinary ascent to the top of the world of golf as well as the influences that spawned the development of those virtues. Tiger's accomplishments clearly transcend sport and so does this book. Tiger's message to the world is both powerful and noble—and Alex Tresniowski captures it perfectly: be more, push harder, dream higher, seek perfection in whatever matters most to you, make a difference. And Tiger backs his message up in the reality of his own life.

In spite of all the folklore surrounding Tiger's legendary accomplishments, he most assuredly is not super human. He is simply an ordinary human being who has found a way to break from the pack and expand his ordinary limits in an extraordinary way. Tiger's mind, his body and his spirit are made of the same stuff and engineered in the same way all of ours is. We thrill in his victories, marvel at his feats and are proud that he is one of us. But the real value in the story and accomplishments of Tiger Woods is in their ability to challenge what we believe to be possible in our own lives and in their ability to help us better understand what it takes to move from ordinary to extraordinary as human beings.

PREFACE

EIGHT SPRINGS AGO, Tiger Woods rocked the golf world with his historic 12-stroke win at the Masters, a victory he calls "the greatest golfing highlight I've ever had in my life." Since then, he has taken the outsized expectations heaped on him and, remarkably, exceeded them. Today, at 29, he is arguably the most famous and popular athlete on the planet.

And he's only getting started.

When all is said and done, however, I believe Tiger's legacy will be less about golf than about how much he helped people improve their lives. He has already helped millions of children through the Tiger Woods Foundation and other charitable enterprises he runs with his father, Earl Woods. Yet it is through the example of his conduct on the golf course that Tiger can have the greatest impact on others, provided we truly open our eyes to what he is doing out there. That is the goal of this book—to examine the many positive attributes that power Tiger's golf and translate them into lessons we can all use to improve ourselves. Forget about learning how to hit a lob wedge—we're talking about the secrets to a happier, more fulfilling life.

I have never spoken to Tiger Woods about these virtues and cannot say he necessarily believes in or endorses them. Tiger has always preferred to let his golf game do his talking for him. But I have discussed these virtues with Tiger's father, Earl. He heartily agrees that Tiger's actions and demeanor provide a wealth of life lessons that anyone can absorb, and he has generously shared his views and insights with me for this book. I have also interviewed all of Tiger's golf coaches during his formative years, top golf analysts such as Gary McCord, David Feherty, Roger Maltbie, Jim Huber and Bobby Clampett, plus performance experts like Dr. Jim Loehr, author of the best-selling *The Power of Full Engagement*. All of them enthusiastically provided original commentary for this book, believing, as I do, that Tiger Woods offers us a rare and wonderful chance to witness—and emulate—true greatness.

This is not a traditional sports book, nor does it contain slick motivational jargon. It is a book about how the way we think determines the way we live. And about how we can find powerful inspiration in the unlikeliest of heroes—a guy who hits a little white ball with a stick. All it requires is that you join me in taking a little walk with Tiger. I hope you get as much out of the journey as I have.

Alex Tresniowski
New York City
March, 2005

ACKNOWLEDGMENTS

Thanks, first and foremost, to Tiger Woods, for the inspirational example of his excellence and dedication. Thank you, also, to his father, Earl Woods, for his warmth and wisdom. Thank you to Tiger's wonderful teachers—Rudy Duran, John Anselmo, Don Crosby and Wally Goodwin—and to those clever fellows who watch Tiger for a living: David Feherty, Gary McCord, Bobby Clampett, Roger Maltbie and Jim Huber. Thank you to the eloquent Sidney Matthews and the exceptional Dr. Jim Loehr. Thank you to Dr. T.J. Dorsey, Anthony Phipps Jr., Angel Gonzalez, Jacob Washington, Corrine Kahn and her parents Noreen and Tom, Stacy Stark, Emily Anderson, Steve Bowen, Tom Strong, Kevin Sullivan and everyone else who helped and encouraged me.

Thank you to everyone at PEOPLE—to the kind and generous Martha Nelson, the endlessly supportive Jack Friedman, the incredible Betsy Gleick, and particularly to my fellow Tigerphile, Cutler Durkee. Thank you, of course, to the lovely Susan Schindehette, the best writer I know. Thanks to my pal Steve Daly; to Frank Weimann, the dealmaker; to Andrew Stuart, the gambler; to Greg Jones, for seeing what I saw. Thanks to Mark Apovian, for fixing my grip. Thanks to Emily, Gracie, Humbolt, Jessie, Jordan, Sam, Willie and Zach, for being so much fun. Thank you to my mother, Cecilia, for making me a writer, and to my great family for putting up with me. Finally, thank you with all my heart to Lorraine Stundis, who inspires me every day. You're my hero.

PART ONE:
IT'S ALL THERE
"I AM AT PEACE"

THE MORNING SPOKE, AND IT SAID TO TIGER WOODS: *Everything in Place.* He had his clubs in the trunk and his Stanford cap on his head and his lucky red shirt on his back and, in the pocket of his perfectly creased pants, a freshly minted State of California drivers license. In his hands, the wheel of the rental car: power, precision, control. "Normally I would drive Tiger to play," says his father, Earl Woods, recalling that special morning in the summer of 1994. "But he had just got his license, so he was driving and I was in the passenger's seat. First time he ever drove himself to a tournament."

And there was more: the sun was bright, the sky a poem, the open road a promise of endless possibility. But still—Tiger was a teenager, and what do teenagers know of such things as harmony and balance and the unseen forces of the universe? What can they know of these things?

And then Tiger said what he said and gave his father goose bumps. It wasn't just what he said, it was that he said anything at all. Never before had Tiger uttered a single word on the way to an event. From the moment he and his father began their drives to the time they arrived at the course, Tiger would sit in silence, staring straight ahead for mile after mile. "He was always in a zone before playing," says Earl Woods. "Never said a word, not once." This day, though, was different; this morning was special. They were on their way to the Royal Oaks Country Club in Vancouver, Washington, where Tiger was in the 36-hole final of the Pacific Northwest Amateur Championship. His opponent: Ted Snavely, a senior at the University of Oregon, the Pac-10 Player of the Year and his state's amateur champ. Tiger Woods, skinny as a six-iron, was four years younger and barely out of high school. On that day, perhaps the last such day, Tiger was the underdog. Yet Earl Woods did not give him a pep talk nor offer any words of advice. He knew better than to say anything at all.

Father and son rode in silence, just as they always had. And then, out of the blue, Tiger spoke.

"Pop?"

"What?"

"I am at peace."

That was it. Nothing more. Neither Tiger nor his father said anything else during the ride. "It was not an expression I had ever used," says Earl, "so I have no idea where it came from." Not much later, at Royal Oaks, it became clear what Tiger had meant. On the first tee, a tight dogleg right, he chose an iron and slashed a perfect drive, and with that he was off and running. At the end of the first 18 holes, Ted Snavely was a solid one under par. Yet he still trailed Tiger by eight. Tiger had gone out in an astounding *nine under par.*

A half-hour lunch break, then back to the course, and then a birdie, and an eagle, and two more birdies, and then the match was over. "Ted made a lot of pars and a couple of birdies, but at some point he was just along for the ride," remembers Steve Bowen, the head pro at Royal Oaks and the referee for the match. "Tiger pretty much chewed him up." Earl Woods, who carried his son's bag in the morning after Tiger's regular caddy called in sick, says, "I will never forget the way Tiger played that day. Nine under after 18, and then he closes the kid out. It was really something to see."

Yet more than the nearly flawless golf—more than Tiger's first masterful victory as an adult—Earl Woods will always remember what his son said to him that morning in the rental car. "It was his way of telling me, '*It's all there.*' When I realized what he meant, boy, the hair on the back of my neck stood up. He was just 18 years old."

I am at peace. It would be another three years before Tiger said those same words to his father again, on a warm April evening just before the start of the 1997 Masters. This time, Tiger was a rookie professional golfer with three wins in his first few months on tour. He was by far the most promising young golfer to appear in years, and likely decades—maybe even ever.

But this was the Masters, the most exacting of golf's four major championships. And Tiger, at the still tender age of 21, was surely too young and too inexperienced to stroll onto the fearsome Augusta fairways and make much of an impression on the leader board. Only a year earlier, when he played in the Masters as an amateur while cramming for college exams, Tiger had not even made the cut. His time would come, no one doubted that, but surely his time was not now.

But then, in a rented condo off Wheeler Road in Augusta, Georgia, Tiger pulled his father aside and said it again: *I am at peace.* "It became his way of telling me that everything is as it should be, that he feels in tune with the universe," says Earl. "He does not say it often. But when he does, I know that he is on his game."

That weekend, Tiger won the Masters by a record 12 strokes and forever changed the way his sport is played.

Tiger Woods traffics in the transcendent, the extraordinary, the absurd. At his best, he has been a summoner of shots that astound the most cynical minds, a conjuror of feats that make a mockery of logic. He has shattered the boundaries of reasonable expectation, inspiring not only his fans but also his competitors to overhaul their assumptions about what can and cannot be achieved. He exists so far beyond the realm of the common that one young fan who came upon him at a golf course asked his mother if Tiger is real. More than any other athlete of his time, Tiger has reconfigured what is possible to accomplish in his sport, condensing generations of progress into just a third of a career. "He is like a comet shooting across the sky—you want to be able to tell your grandchildren that you saw him," says Sidney Matthew, the noted golf historian and author of *Life & Times of Bobby Jones.* "He is perceived as being able to do things that mortal men cannot, and that's why people are drawn to him—they want to be a piece of that history."

Indeed, Tiger's finest achievements have played out like science fiction. He won the 2000 British Open at storied St. Andrews by eight strokes, but even more remarkable was that he played four rounds—a total of 269 strokes—without hitting a single ball into any of the course's 112 bunkers, devilishly situated to snare all manner of errant and not-so-errant shots. Given the erratic character of that rolling links—stuffed with bumps and moguls that veer balls off course and into the deep sand pits—missing every one of the bunkers seems downright mystical.

Similarly, Tiger won the 1997 Masters at Augusta National without requiring more than two putts on any green. Again, considering the porcelain greens that give Augusta its primary bite, avoiding a single three-putt is not merely extraordinary, it's borderline extraterrestrial.

Then there was his victory at the 2003 Bay Hill Invitational, when Tiger fell ill before the fourth round after eating spaghetti prepared by his then-girlfriend Elin Nordegren. He vomited several times during the final round but did not card a single bogey and won—*by 11 strokes.* And what about his unforgettable next-to-last shot at the 2001 NEC Invitational, when—unable to see the 18th green in the fading twilight—Tiger struck a blind, 180-yard pitching wedge that landed less than a foot from the cup.

These and other lore-making moments have, in their accumulation, accustomed Tiger's fans to his greatness without robbing them of the thrill of his mastery. TV ratings soar even when Tiger's leads are so large, his victories such forgone conclusions, that fans are essentially tuning in to watch a coronation. "He is an ordinary human being who has demonstrated a pathway to the extraordinary," says Dr. Jim Loehr, author of the best-selling *The Power of Full Engagement* and a performance psychologist who works with top professional athletes. "What he has demonstrated has rocked every serious competitor on the PGA tour. He may be starting in golf, but I think he is transcending golf. He is redefining the way in which we see the world."

Of course, Tiger does not perform at such astonishing levels all the time. Golf is such a fickle sport—and life so full of vagaries—that no amount of practice and preparation can produce consistently flawless results. In his eight years as a professional, he has even endured two lengthy dips in his fortunes—slumps, some might say—during which he has often seemed like merely a very good player. Yet Tiger's talents have also allowed him to win tournaments and play spectacular golf even when he is not firing on all cylinders. "If Tiger plays well, it is a matter of who is going to finish second that week, and all the guys know that," says former pro golfer and CBS golf analyst Bobby Clampett. "And the thing is, Tiger often doesn't play all that well and still finds a way to win. And that drives the other players crazy."

Early in his career, Tiger referred to his peak playing level as his "A game," and often boasted of winning some events with only his "B" or even his "C game." He stopped ranking his performances alphabetically once he realized veteran golfers disliked being thumped by a kid claiming to be at less than full capacity. But Tiger has found other ways to discuss what everyone now knows is true: that when he has everything in place—when he is at peace—he can raise his game to new heights and become essentially unbeatable. "To me, it's all about balance," Tiger explained in 2002. "Your entire life, you're always working to keep everything in balance, because the more harmony there is, the smoother life goes."

Tiger's pursuit and frequent attainment of this blissful state offers us a rare and wonderful window into peak performance. Some might argue that Tiger's play is so spectacular, his shots so magnificent, that he is simply some kind of freak—an inimitable golfing machine. But the beauty of Tiger Woods is that by hitting such amazing shots, he shows us precisely what is possible. By playing superior golf, Tiger manifests what lays dormant in so many people—a great and untapped potential to achieve more than they ever dreamed they could.

That is the reason people with no prior interest in golf—grandmothers, housewives, skateboarding teens—find themselves mesmerized by Tiger Woods: they are responding instinctively to his mastery, and to the many virtuous characteristics inherent in his play. "People who don't know a putter from a garden hoe will watch Tiger to see him do something phenomenal," says Sidney Matthew. "There is a great detachment in the world today, and all of us want to connect to something and make ourselves relevant. And the way to do that is to identify with a hero who connects us to the world. A hero who gives us joy and happiness and makes us say: 'Yes, I am worthy, I have what it takes, and, yes, I too can slay the dragon.'"

This book is not a conventional biography of Tiger Woods. There are many fine books that focus on his upbringing, and the memorable details of his life—how he hopped out of his high chair at ten months to imitate his father's golf swing; how he learned to keep score in relation to par before he learned how to count; how his father used military tactics to instill mental toughness in his son. Nor will this book delve into Tiger's personal life away from golf. Off the course, he is untouchable, zealously guarding his privacy and projecting a public persona that is, by design, bland and boring. "There's a lot of things besides golf that Tiger likes to do, but he has managed to do them without being photographed, which is remarkable," says the delightful CBS golf commentator David Feherty, a former top player. "You never see him in the tabloids—never. My theory is that he's actually a short fat white guy living in a cave and waiting for a signal in the sky to put on his Tiger suit."

Rather, *Tiger Virtues* is an invitation to approach the golf of Tiger

Woods in a new way, which in turn will broaden your perception of what is and isn't possible. I have never met Tiger, though I have spoken with his father, his golf coaches, his colleagues and many others who know him well, and as a sportswriter for PEOPLE Magazine I have written about Tiger many times. First and foremost, I am, like most of you, a fan—perhaps a fanatic. Captivated the first time I saw Tiger on television in 1994, I have traveled to several tournaments to watch him play, and I have missed not a single one of his televised performances since he turned pro in 1996. I have built whole weekends around savoring each and every one of his swings, and I have preserved and revisited his most thrilling wins on tape. I have, like his millions of admirers around the world, marveled at his exploits and felt exhilarated by his expertise. I have noticed a bounce in my step during weeks when Tiger plays; I have felt the earth slip back on its axis on Sundays when he wins. Along the way, I wondered why I was so drawn to Tiger—why, after a lifetime of rooting for underdogs, I found myself giddily pulling for the ultimate front-runner. I felt compelled to understand why Tiger so moved and inspired me. I needed to know what exactly was happening here.

And so it was that I began this book and reached my simple conclusion—that in the golf of Tiger Woods lie the secrets of the universe. Even a casual analyst of his play can discern that Tiger isn't just mindlessly knocking the dimples off of golf balls. His approach has an obvious cerebral and spiritual dimension, a clear grounding in something deep and powerful. In fact, Tiger sticks to a handful of principles drawn from several disciplines, most notably his father Earl's training as a Green Beret and his mother Tida's Buddhist beliefs.

This latter influence—the basic tenets of Buddhism—is easily the least scrutinized aspect of Tiger's greatness, perhaps because the Eastern religion is so foreign to most of his fans. The impact of Buddhism on Tiger's golf game "has been underestimated," says Sidney Matthew. "I think Tiger draws a lot from it, and has learned to harness it to his advantage." John Anselmo, Woods' coach from the time Tiger was ten to when he was 17, agrees that "growing up in Buddhism really helped him. I didn't realize what it was all about back then, but the concentration and meditation—Tiger was doing that at a young age. He was much quieter and more self-possessed than the other kids, no question." While Tiger, whose mother was born in Thailand, does not dwell on the influence of Buddhism on his game, he has repeatedly acknowledged its role in shaping his character. "If there's anyone who instilled discipline in me, it's my mother," he revealed in 2001. "The Asian heritage is a lot more disciplined than what we experience here in the States, and that was the culture in the household I was raised."

Tiger's blending of Buddhism and other influences into a seamless performance ethic makes him a rare and valuable role model. An absolute wealth of wisdom can be gleaned from his actions and words. This book does not purport to know what is in Tiger's mind when he plays or to attribute his success solely to the virtues herein. It does not pretend to have inside information about his specific methods. While Tiger has discussed his regimen from time to time and to various degrees, for the most part he keeps the details of how he prepares to himself. But it is in his speech and his conduct—the things we are privy to—that we can find Tiger's message to us: try harder, be better, dream higher, be your own hero. I believe that watching Tiger play golf, and paying close attention to how he goes about his business, can impart key lessons—lessons that can help us improve not only our golf but our performance in any endeavor. Emulating Tiger can help people become not only better putters or chippers but, of far more consequence, better people who enjoy a higher quality of life.

Indeed, to disregard the example of such a masterful performer is to not only waste a wonderful opportunity but to deny a basic human impulse. "No nobler feeling than this of admiration for one higher than himself dwells in the breast of man," the great English thinker Thomas Carlyle wrote in his seminal 1841 work *On Heroes, Hero-Worship and the Heroic in History*. Or as Michael Gelb had it in his brilliant *How to Think Like Leonardo da Vinci*, when he quoted Giorgio Vasari's writings on Leonardo: "Heaven sometimes sends us beings who represent not humanity alone but divinity itself, so that taking them as our models and imitating them, our minds and the best of our intelligence may approach the highest celestial spheres."

I believe that Tiger Woods is just such a role model. "Tiger is Mozart, he's Einstein, he's a genius at golf," agrees Rudy Duran, Tiger's first golf coach, who worked with him for six years starting when Tiger was four. "But anyone can maximize their individual abilities if they do the things he does." The man who knows Tiger better than anyone feels the same way. "Tiger lives by these principles and they work for him," says his father Earl. "And if other people do the same things, they will work for them."

Fear not, however, that *Tiger Virtues* is some obtuse self-help book full of empty jargon and annoying exercises. It is nothing of the sort. It is simply one fan's appreciation of a special athlete, driven by an enthusiasm for the many aspects of his greatness. Those who make the leap and accept its premise may not achieve the impossible, as Tiger has, but, like Tiger, they very well may begin to believe that they can. "When Tiger was four or five, he had this idea of a perfect round of golf," says Earl. "He would come to me and say, 'Dad, some-day I'm going to shoot 18 birdies.' That was always his objective."

"I believe that, one of these days when everything is perfect, Tiger is going to do it," says Earl. "Why not?"

PART TWO:
THE TAO OF TIGER

TWENTY-FIVE CENTURIES BEFORE TIGER WOODS was born, a man of uncommon demeanor arrived at the place where he would commence his mission. Transformed by intense, ritualistic training, he sat with a group of curious people who would become the first to witness his exceptional poise and grace. The man would soon be known to his followers as The Buddha, one of the most influential teachers of all time. And the place where he began his mission, near the holy city of Benares in India, was a lovely place called Deer Park.

Two thousand five hundred years later, a man of uncommon demeanor arrived at the place where he would commence his mission. Transformed by intense, ritualistic training, he walked among a group of curious people who would witness his exceptional poise and grace. The man was known to his followers as Tiger Woods, one of the most influential athletes of all time. And the place where he began his mission, not far from Milwaukee, Wisconsin, was a lovely place called *Deer Park*.

An amazing coincidence, to be sure—or is it? That both the Buddha and his spiritual descendent Tiger Woods would make their debuts at a place called Deer Park (actually, the full name of the course where Tiger played his first pro event is Brown Deer Park) seems serendipitously appropriate—a wonderful cosmic wink. For we have, in these kindred souls separated by 25 centuries, two extraordinary teachers of an enlightened way of life.

Hold on, you say? Are we equating a prophet whose wisdom has sustained a global religion for nearly three millennium to a guy who makes his living hitting lob wedges? Well, no. But there is merit to the notion that Tiger, in his own way, may be able to do what the Buddha did—change the world. "He is the Chosen One," proclaimed his father Earl Woods, the first to advance the notion at a 1996 charity awards dinner. "He will transcend this game and bring to the world a humanitarianism which has never been known before. The world will be a better place to live in by virtue of his existence and his presence."

At the time, Earl was ridiculed for his eye-rolling prediction. "When he referred to his son as some kind of messiah I thought, 'Gee, that's a really big word,'" says Wally Goodwin, coach of the Stanford University golf team during the two years Tiger was there. But today—eight years into the Tiger Woods Era—eyes aren't rolling anymore. "Now you have to say that Earl was 95 percent correct," says Goodwin. "Tiger is having a huge impact on people. Anyone who watches him can learn from Tiger. They better learn from Tiger. And not just about golf, but about everything."

Put simply, Tiger has not only transformed the sport of golf, he has provided a template for transforming people's lives. Never mind that he chases a little ball around fancy country clubs; what he does matters far less than how he does it. His performances have so consistently pushed the envelope of perception, Tiger often seems like an emissary from another dimension, here to debunk the logic and limits that govern our lives. "Some of the golf shots he hits, you know he's the only human being on the face of the earth who could hit that shot," says former PGA star and NBC analyst Roger Maltbie. "It becomes ridiculous at times as an announcer to try to put into words what you just witnessed. After a while you feel like, 'Gee, are people getting tired of hearing me deify this guy?'"

From the beginning, Tiger's galleries sensed that they were watching someone special—that being in his presence made you part of the phenomenon. Yes, Tiger was an African-American in a sport nearly devoid of minorities, but that would have been a mere novelty were it not for the level of his play. His appeal had much more to do with performance than pigment. The thousands drawn to Brown Deer Park to watch Tiger's debut at the 1996 Greater Milwaukee Open approached him "with a mixture of giddiness and reverence," says Tom Strong, then the tournament's director. Along the first fairway—which 20-year-old Tiger split with a soaring drive and a playful waggle of his tongue— "there were just walls of people from one end to the other; everybody wanted to be a part of this," says Strong. "I think everyone wanted to know what it feels like to stand up and hit a golf ball 340 yards down the middle."

The clarion call, however, came later, on the par 3, 202-yard 14th hole. "I tried to punch a 6-iron under the wind, but it went higher than I wanted,"Tiger would later say. "The ball hit on the green and kicked left and I said, 'That should be close.'" Halfway across the golf course, Tom Strong was stepping out of his office when he heard a sound like thunder. "There's a certain roar when someone makes birdie, but this was totally different," he recalls. "I said right away, 'there's only one thing a roar like that could be for, and that's Tiger Woods making a one.'"

Indeed, Tiger's thrilling hole-in-one—in his first round as a pro and under the intense pressure of huge expectations—heralded the arrival of something not quite ordinary. Cometh the hour, they say, cometh the man.

From then on, jaws just kept dropping. There was the cloud-scraping iron that tickled the cup and beat golf's best player, Tom Lehman, at the 1996 Mercedes Championship. "It's almost like trying to hold off the inevitable," a dazed Lehman would say of challenging Tiger, then playing in only his ninth pro event. "Like bailing water out of a sinking boat." There was the 12-stroke thrashing of dumfounded veterans at the 1997 Masters. "We're all human beings here, but there's no chance humanly possible that Tiger is just going to lose this tournament," Colin Montgomerie, an elite player, said in surrender after only three rounds.

There was the spun-in eagle to power a four-stroke comeback at the 2000 AT&T Pro-Am; the ridiculous bunker shot over water and into wind to win the 2000 Canadian Open; the trance-like procession to a 15-shot victory at the 2000 U.S. Open, the first of four straight major titles; the chased-in birdie on a playoff hole to steal the 2000 PGA. Impossible shots made possible, cartoonish deeds rendered human, the drama of realized greatness delivered as sports theater. "To me, he's right at the top of the list with Ali and Joe Namath as far as electric, spectacular characters," says TNT's superb golf essayist Jim Huber. "And yet, with Tiger, there is so much more than just a flash of greatness. You can tell he is going to be around for a while. He thrives on his place in history."

Let us look back, then, on what will likely be the first third of Tiger's historic career. In just his first eight full seasons, Tiger—who turned 29 on December 30, 2004, and who, barring injury, should be able to play at a high level into his forties—is roughly halfway to breaking some of his sport's most revered records. He won eight major titles much more quickly than Jack Nicklaus, whose record 18 major wins represents Tiger's Holy Grail. With 40 PGA tour wins, he's ahead of schedule to eclipse Sam Snead's all-time mark of 81. In his first seven years, Arnold Palmer won 27 of his first 205 events, or around 13 percent. Tiger won 38 of 142 tournaments, an unprecedented 27 percent rate of victory. (He finished in the top 10 a remarkable 64 percent of the time). In 1999, Tiger claimed 52 percent of all the prize money he competed for, and nearly twice as much as the next biggest money winner. He was ranked No. 1 in the world for 264 consecutive weeks, a new record; he did not finish out of the money in any of 129 consecutive events through the 2004 PGA, also a new record.

These and other achievements have made Tiger the most popular athlete on the planet, and one of the four or five most recognizable people in the world. He has been named the most important minority athlete, as well as the athlete with the broadest global reach. His skills and the recognition they've brought have put him in a unique position to advance an agenda. But so far, Tiger has avoided using his pulpit to make any statements about race or politics. "I play golf for selfish reasons," he has said. "To win tournaments." At the same time he is clearly aware of—and comfortable with—the fame Earl Woods predicted his son would use to change the world. "I've always known where I want to go," he said in 1996. "I've never let anything deter me. This is my purpose. It will unfold."

Eight years later, it has unfolded—his purpose is to help people lead better lives. To change the world for the better, to make us dream bigger, to show everyone that anything is possible.

It is a central tenet of Buddhism that anyone can be a Buddha— that all of us can shine a light for others to follow. One does not even need to know that he is a Buddha to be a Buddha, so powerful is the speech and conduct of an Enlightened One. The Buddha himself walked on water and traveled to heaven and back. And while Tiger's highlight reel isn't quite as impressive, he has earned our attention nonetheless. "Tiger has always been a teacher," says his father Earl. "He is teaching things by just being himself. It is everyone's prerogative if they want to emulate him. He is not going to push anything on you, but if you want to learn from Tiger, you can."

In mythological terms, Tiger is fulfilling the role of the hero, pushing the boundaries of consciousness and blazing a trail to lead others out of darkness. "The hero learns to experience the supernormal range of human spiritual life and then comes back with a message," the late scholar Joseph Campbell explained in his brilliant *The Power of Myth*. "We have only to follow the thread of the hero path, and where we had thought to find an abomination, we shall find a god."

When Earl Woods told reporters Tiger would have a greater impact than even the Buddha himself, he was envisioning the supernormal message Campbell described being broadcast from the global platform his son would surely command. After all, the Buddha wasn't on television 25 weekends a year. The combination of Tiger's excellence and his immense reach makes him a uniquely compelling role model. "Tiger is pushing the window of extraordinary in every way possible," says Dr. Jim Loehr. "We all yearn to make a difference, and that is the nuclear material of life. But so many times, the gears get corroded and covered up and then we don't have a destination point. Now, we can just look at Tiger and see that what he is doing is giving him a huge return. And that can be true of all of us, if we make the kind of commitment Tiger has."

All well and good, you might say, but what sort of hero stumbles into golf, the sport of country clubs, Sansabelt slacks and Tim Conway's Dorf? Achilles had the Trojan War—Tiger has the Booz-Allen Classic? In fact, golf ranks as the most spiritual and cerebral of sports, and the most like life itself. There are no walls, no nets, no lanes or lines, only trees and lakes and gently rolling hills. There is no jumping of hurdles or hoisting of dumbbells or running in circles, only people walking purposefully from point to point, much as we do everyday. There are no teams or uniforms or shoulder pads or mouth guards, only individuals facing obstacles, falling or rising on their merits, using their wiles to get out of trouble—again, like life.

Golf is based on honor and steeped in tradition; in what other sport do players police themselves? It places a premium on mental toughness and resolve, and offers a plentitude of psychologically challenging situations. After all, the golfer is not really competing against other golfers; ultimately, he is competing against himself. "That feeling of solitude and self-reliance enhanced the game's attraction to me," Tiger has acknowledged. "It always comes down to how well you know yourself." Stripped of clocks and bells and buzzers and other artificial trappings, golf lays bare the soul and the psyche like very few other sports. "Bobby Jones tapped into this when he was asked why golf is so captivating," says Sidney Matthew. "He said in the space of a few hours, you can face the gamut of life's experiences without having to repair a personality or bury a corpse at the end of the day. You can be the clown in a comedy, the actor in a melodrama, the dogged victim of inexorable fate, all within the space of a few hours. Golf is a microcosm of life."

The opportunities are there, then, to demonstrate positive attributes and a mastery over one's mind, and it is beyond question that Tiger has done just that. More than his monster drives and swashbuckler attitude, it is the collective power of Tiger's many virtuous traits—manifest in his aura of strength and majesty—that has lured so many new fans to the game. "When I was in high school, golf wasn't really a cool sport," says Roger Maltbie. "You were a geek if you played golf. Now, thanks to Tiger, golfers are viewed as athletes. And that is a sign of the impact he is having on kids." Besides converting youngsters who had been more likely to pick up a broom than a golf club, Tiger has also worked his magic on the older set. "My mother is almost 80, and she can't pull herself away from the TV when Tiger plays," says Jim Huber. "She'll tune into every round and watch him endlessly. I'll call her on Sundays and she'll say, 'Did you see Tiger, did you see what he did?'"

Most noticeably, Tiger has shattered the image of golf as a homogenous sport. He has such a grab bag of blood in his veins, he's a walking Bennetons ad. "Tiger has Thai, African, Chinese, American Indian and European blood," his mother Tida once said. "He is the Universal Child." Because of this he can be a stand-in for just about everyone: young or old, black or white, male or female, hipster or geek. Consider the slogans in his TV ads: "I am Tiger Woods," intoned a multi-colored array of fans in one early spot; "Go ahead," urged another, "be a Tiger." Oprah Winfrey called Tiger "America's son." Everyone can identify with him, because everyone *is* him. "The galleries are definitely younger now, definitely more eclectic," says CBS's inimitable analyst Gary McCord. "We always had the Abercrombie and Fitch crowd, but now we have tank tops and tattoos and wolverine boots and just about everything. It's a sociological potpourri out there. And it's really fun and exciting to see that."

Yet Tiger has inspired much more than increased ticket sales. The example of his excellence transformed the game of golf at every level. "We now have guys who can play at a much higher level than what Tiger faced when he was here," says his coach at Western High School, Don Crosby. "Because of Tiger, golf gets some of the better athletes instead of football or baseball. That's the case not only here in California, but all across the country. He changed high school golf in a very short time. And he did the same in college."

His impact on the PGA tour was not immediate, as it took seasoned professionals a while to lower their defenses. The great and noble sport of golf had done just fine without him, thank you very much, and what could its veteran players possibly learn from a kid who didn't even have stubble yet? Soon enough they came to view Tiger's methods much like one views a runaway train: hop aboard or get out of the way. David Feherty describes the four stages of coping with Tiger. "It starts off as anger, and moves on to jealousy, and then, gradually, if you're being honest with yourself, it's admiration," says Feherty. "Eventually you end up awestruck just like everybody else."

Tiger's dominance initially had a negative effect on some players, bulldozing their confidence and sending them scurrying to golf psychologists. Ernie Els, the No. 1 player in the world for eight weeks in 1998 before losing several head-to-head duels with Tiger, asked sports shrink Jos Vanstiphout to help him feel less dazzled by his rival.

"When Tiger returned in 2000 his physique was incredible, his swing was perfect," Els once gushed. "He was unreal." Davis Love III, the victim in Tiger's first victory and many more after that, dialed up a few sessions with positive thinker Dr. Bob Rotella.

Eventually, though, it became clear that Tiger's supremacy—and attendant popularity—was helping more than hurting. Stunned into action by Tiger, golfers of all rank and skill have since come into their own. "There's a large group [of us] who have stepped forward and lifted their games," Els said in 2004, the year he passed Tiger in golf's world rankings. What's more, bigger crowds and higher ratings mean more prize money, which benefits everyone. Pros played for a total of $69 million in 1996; by 2001 it was $180 million. Life was better with Tiger around.

Few enjoyed a bigger bounty than Tiger's friend and Florida neighbor Mark O'Meara. A terrific touring pro for nearly two decades, he played in dozens of majors without ever winning one. That is, until Tiger turned to him in 1997 and said, "I don't understand why you haven't won a major. You can do it." That gentle jab in the ribs, along with his exposure to Tiger's intense work ethic and the advantage of playing practice rounds against the world's top golfer, profoundly inspired Mark O'Meara. At the age of 41, he won not one but two majors, turning a so-so career into a stellar one. "Tiger's enthusiasm, his youth, his competitiveness kind of turned me around a little bit," he would say.

This is what Tiger does—he wakes people to their potential. His brilliance rubs off on those exposed to him, both on and off the course. One of the more stunning examples of his far-reaching influence is the Tiger Woods Effect, the name given to his apparent ability to move the nation's stock market. On Mondays following weekends when Tiger played in 2000 and 2001, the Dow Jones industrial average inevitably rose, a formula that held for 21 straight events over more than thirteen months. Conversely, the stock market dropped 80 percent of the time on Mondays following weekends when Tiger stayed home. Some analysts speculated Tiger's affluent fans carried their good feelings about him into their Monday trading; others believed stockbrokers were whipped into Tiger-like frenzies by their hero, producing market rallies. Either way, it is difficult to think of another athlete whose excellence has served as such an inspiration in so many different ways.

Motivating Mark O'Meara and firing up stockbrokers are swell achievements, but Tiger is focused firmly on a different demographic. From the very start of his pro career, he has insisted that the ultimate beneficiaries of his success must be underprivileged children. In 1997 he launched the Tiger Woods Foundation, a charity that has raised many millions to teach golf to inner-city kids. "A lot of guys go their whole careers and don't focus on helping and giving back," says Gary McCord. "And Tiger did that from the very beginning. The first thing he did was start a program to help kids."

He has also hosted several youth golf clinics, laying his hand on a shoulder here, propping up an elbow there and always spreading his message of dreaming big and working hard. At one clinic in Orlando, Tiger's reception was so spirited "it was almost as if God was in the children's midst," Dr. T. J. Dorsey, founder and director of the Orlando Minority Youth Golf Association, observed at the time.

Today, Dr. Dorsey says, "I think Tiger has impacted these kids in the greatest possible way. He has had an influence on all kids, but especially minority kids, who now have a hero they can look up to. Those who are fortunate enough to get close to him, you can see it is a memorable experience for them. They go for what he's saying hook, line and sinker. You can see them just light up." Twelve-year-old Anthony Phipps, Jr., a nifty young golfer who models himself on Tiger, was lucky enough to have his idol work with him one-on-one at a recent clinic. Anthony's goals for the future? "First I want to go to Stanford, where Tiger went," he says. "Then I want to study to be a lawyer. And then I want to try and play golf."

Think Tiger's message is getting through? "The Foundation is a lot more important than winning tournaments," he said in 2004. "That has always been the case, even before I turned pro—to have an impact away from golf." In other words, we have not yet seen the full and true measure of Tiger's gift; the really amazing stuff is still to come. "Right now he's trying to be better than Jack Nicklaus, and when he finally accomplishes that, we'll see what he's really all about," says his old swing coach John Anselmo. "I told Earl Woods that I just want to live long enough to see what Tiger can do."

Look, no one is saying that Tiger Woods is perfect. Certainly, he has never said it himself. He is not a god or an angel or anyone's dream of goodness—he is flesh and blood, thoroughly human, full of flaws. He has a temper, and a nasty one at that: there was the time he mangled eight putters after a bad round of golf. He may love mankind, but he certainly doesn't love everyone. "There are a lot of guys on tour I can't stand," he once said. And, boy, can he curse. Most famously he failed to notice a boom mike on the 18th tee during the 2000 U.S. Open at Pebble Beach and, after pulling a drive into the Pacific Ocean, unleashed a self-criticism so profane it had three different unprintable words in it (he also once cursed on live TV during a meaningless Monday night event). Ghandi, this guy ain't.

At the same time, Tiger's everyday conduct suggests he is already a long way down the road to enlightenment. He appears capable of tapping his potential more readily than others, of summoning his very best in moments when nothing less will do. Should this not make him an object of fascination to us? Do we not envy his passion, his purpose, his pride? Is he not a brighter light in a murky world? Maybe not the Chosen One, but the one we choose to emulate? "You have this ability," Nelson Mandela told Tiger when the two met in South Africa. "Do some good with it."

There is goodness there already, in the golf of Tiger Woods. It is only a matter of paying attention.

When Tiger was five, he asked his father to buy him a tricycle. Earl Woods told his son he had to think about it. Every day, Tiger would ask for that tricycle, and every day Earl would say he was still thinking. "This went on for a couple of months," remembers Earl. "Until one day I finally said, 'Okay, you can have that tricycle.'"

Tiger's reaction? Did he jump up and down with joy? Demand to go buy it? Ask when he could expect to have it? "I got absolutely no reaction at all," says Earl. "Tiger just turned around, walked into the next room and did something else. And I wondered, 'Why did he do that?' Then it dawned on me—Tiger trusted me. Most kids would have wanted details—when will I get it, what kind? But for Tiger, it was enough to know I had said I would get it for him. That's when I knew I had his trust."

If you are searching for the roots of Tiger's greatness, it's right there in the tricycle tale. His parents Earl and Tida raised their only son with an abundance of love and attention, guiding him towards not just supremacy in golf, but supremacy as a human being. Early on, they succeeded in instilling a series of deep and lasting values— respect, perseverance, responsibility, trust. They laid the foundation that enabled Tiger to rise to a towering height, and gave him the confidence he needed to stay there. The love and integrity of Tiger's parents provided him with an enormous advantage as he made his way in the world. "They both had a part to play in Tiger's life and they both took great care to do it," says his Stanford coach Wally Goodwin. "And that made it a pleasure to be around him."

Earl and Tida brought different sensibilities—but equal commitment—to the task of raising Tiger. Earl spent 20 years in the military and served two tours of duty in Vietnam, rising to the rank of Lieutenant Colonel in the Green Berets. While stationed in Bangkok in 1967, he met Kultida Punsawad, a Thai-born secretary in the U.S. Army Office. Earl had been married before and had fathered three children, but today he admits he was not a particularly good husband or father. The second time around, though, would be different. He and Tida wed in 1969; six years later Tiger arrived. The birth name

Tida designed for their son was Eldrick—the "E" for Earl and the "K" for Kultida, symbolic of their vow to always surround their son. The nickname—Tiger—came from Earl, who had bestowed the same moniker on his friend Nguyen Phong, a South Vietnamese soldier who saved Earl's life more than once.

Earl insists he had no master plan for Tiger, beyond shaping him into an exemplary person. The golf thing happened more or less by accident. Earl picked up the game late, at 42, and set up some carpet and a nylon net in the garage of his Cypress, California, home so he could work on his swing. Dozens of golf records became officially imperiled the day Earl hauled in a wooden high chair so he could practice and watch his kid at the same time. Mesmerized by his father's sessions, ten-month-old Tiger slithered down the high chair one day, grabbed a sawed-off putter, put a ball on the matt and perfectly mimicked his dad's swing. "He almost hit it into the net!" says Earl, still thrilled by the memory. "I was so amazed, I ran to get his mother, and meanwhile Tiger had put down another ball and was doing it again. He was practicing, just like me."

More precocious moments followed: Tiger at two memorizing his dad's work number so he could call and bug him to play; Tiger at four pocketing money from skeptics on the putting green; Tiger at five appearing on national TV as a guest on *The Mike Douglas Show* and *That's Incredible*; Tiger at six scoring his first—and second—holes-in-one; Tiger at 12 breaking par and beating his father for the first time. "When he came to me at four, it was like he was twenty-five in golf terms," says Rudy Duran, who was the head pro at Heartwell Golf Park in Long Beach, California, the day Tida Woods walked in and inquired about private lessons for her son. "I teed up four or five balls and he hit his little 2- wood and he just smacked them off the tee, one after the other. These perfect 80-yard draws. If I hadn't seen it myself, I wouldn't have believed it."

Along the way, Tiger blew right by whole phases of the maturation process—no terrible twos, no adolescent angst, no moody teen years. Never threw a tantrum, never got grounded. Never had a babysitter because his folks liked having him around. He made mistakes, but usually only once, since his parents drilled it into him that every mistake was a lesson in disguise. "When he was young he'd hit a bad shot and pound his club into the ground," says Earl. "I'd ask, 'Was the club the reason you hit a bad shot? The crows in the trees? The wind?' And Tiger would say, 'No, it was me.' That's how he learned to take responsibility for his actions."

Nothing Earl and Tida taught him was trendy or new. All of it had been around. "This isn't a PhD treatise," says Earl. "We weren't reinventing anything." The key was applying their lessons with consistency and care. Once they had Tiger's trust, there was nothing they couldn't teach him. It helped that Tiger, as those who know him note, is one of the great listeners of all time.

This is why he was able to synthesize the two disparate disciplines introduced by his mom and dad. Earl and Tida, the Green Beret and the Buddhist—Mr. Military and Mrs. Meditation. Together they formed a crafty alliance of East and West, a two-front assault on Tiger's consciousness. Much like Tiger's game itself—a seamless blend of power and precision—his indoctrination derived its power from the meshing of two complementary elements. The sum of his education proved far greater than its parts.

Always, the goal was to ensure that Tiger would be strong, psychologically and spiritually. Earl Woods, war veteran, signed up for the former. After much introspection, he decided to take the brutal tactics he had picked up in the military—prisoner-of-war interrogation techniques, mental toughness drills—and use them on his skinny little son. He would bark, 'Out of bounds on the right!' in the middle of Tiger's backswing, or drop his golf bag or jiggle some change or pump the brakes on his cart. He would do this three or four times in a row, then keep still on the fifth swing, rattling Tiger with his silence. Swing after swing, round after round, month after month, the torture continued. Earl called it the Woods Finishing School and he gave his son a safety word—"enough"—that would stop the harassment. Tiger never once used the word. Earl would look for frowns and flinches, but after a while all he saw was smiles. When it was over, he told his boy, "You'll never play anyone who's mentally stronger than you are."' And he was right.

When they weren't on the course, Earl had Tiger listen to subliminal audiotapes. *I will own my destiny, I believe in me*, they intoned. *My will moves mountains . . . my decisions are strong.* Tiger listened to the tapes so often that he wore them out.

Yet it would not be right to think of Earl as a relentless taskmaster. He never forced Tiger to play a round of golf, never pushed him to practice longer or harder. In fact, he had to pull his son off the practice range just to remember what he looked like. What's more, no rule or lesson was ever crammed down Tiger's throat. The mutual trust between father and son meant screaming wasn't necessary. "I never professed that I had the answers to everything," says Earl. "I told Tiger, 'This is the way I see things, and you can use this information anyway you want. If you use all of it or use none of it, that's okay. You know I will love you just the same.'" It is a fundamental notion of Oriental philosophy that a teacher does not teach unless he is asked. Lessons must be willingly received; the student must be ready to accept them.

Tiger did have a drill sergeant for a parent, but it wasn't his mushy old dad. Tida Woods, a disarming combination of steeliness and gentility, was the one who took Tiger's clubs away if she needed to make a point. The one who flicked him on the back of the head if he didn't say "Yes, sir" or "thank you." The one, Tiger has often said, "who taught me how to be disciplined." Not the Lieutenant Colonel—the sweet little lady with the saintly smile.

It was Tida, too, who insisted her son be steeped in the culture and traditions of her native Thailand. This exposed him from an early age to the Buddhist way of life. A religion founded in India in the sixth century B.C., it now has millions of followers around the world. At the gentle heart of the Buddhist faith is a message of great hope— we can, every one of us, be awakened to our true and authentic selves. We are in charge of our own destinies and capable of shaping our world into what we wish it to be.

The Buddhist scriptures strive to foster spiritual fulfillment, eliminate fear and delusions, advance meaningful connections and promote a higher level of self realization. Buddhism provides a path to achieving enlightened consciousness, which very simply means discovering an enduringly positive notion of ourselves. It is one of the loveliest beliefs of Buddhism that we can all become Buddhas, or "ones who are awakened." We need only realize we are much more powerful than we think.

The story of the Buddha himself continues to inspire the religion's devotees. Born Siddhartha Guatama around 563 B.C., he was the son of a wealthy king who bestowed him every material luxury and shielded him from suffering and tragedy. Restless with his life of privilege and tormented by the impermanence of existence, Prince Siddhartha, at age 29, left behind a wife and son to venture into a forest and seek a better understanding of the meaning of existence and death. He burned his clothes, cut off his hair, renounced possessions and lived austerely, training himself, the story goes, to subsist on a single grain of rice a day.

He eventually found a peaceful spot under a sacred tree and commenced a long period of deep meditation, resisting temptations by shutting down his senses and turning completely inward. It was this intense concentration and profound stillness that delivered him to a higher level of consciousness—that allowed him to awaken to the true nature of happiness. As in mythology, which requires the hero to return from his solitary adventure to share the fruits of his journey, the Buddha left his tree and came back to the world. He arrived at Deer Park and found five students who, moved by his radiance, asked him to teach them what he had learned. The Buddha would spend decades passing on his wisdom.

His teachings were recorded in many different scriptures: among them, *The Dhammapada*, a collection of 423 verses believed to have been assembled by disciples of the Buddha in the sixth century B.C. Some of those verses will appear in this book to provide a sense of the power and simplicity of Buddhism's key insights.

The fundamentals of Eastern thinking can also be found in the *Tao Te Ching*, which contains 81 verses devoted to charting a path to higher consciousness. In its lovely pages "there is an answer to each of life's questions, a solution to every predicament, a balm for every wound," writes Brian Browne Walker, a student of Chinese and Taoist philosophy whose exceptional translation of the *Tao Te Ching* is a source for this book. Walker tells us that the author of the *Tao Te Ching*, Lao Tzu, was likely not one man, but rather six Chinese sages who gathered the wisdom of the ages during the Chou Dynasty 26 centuries ago. These two ancient texts are endlessly revealing and wonderfully accessible, and help a great deal in understanding the basics of the philosophy to which young Tiger was exposed.

He had a fine teacher in his mother Tida, who on her first date with Earl Woods insisted she be taken to the Temple of the Reclining Buddha in Bangkok. When their child was born, she followed a Buddhist ritual and began keeping a detailed chart about him. She took the chart with her on her first trip to Thailand with Tiger when he was nine, and showed it to a Buddhist monk. "He said Tiger was going to be a leader," Tida later revealed. "It's like God send angel." A monk in Los Angeles predicted the same thing, Tida has said. Surely this must have brought to mind the story of the Buddha himself. When the Buddha was born, a prophet told his father that the boy would grow up to be a world leader or teacher.

Back in California, Tiger and his mother would travel to a Buddhist temple every year around his birthday, and offer the monks there a present of rice, sugar and salt. It was at the Buddhist temple that Zen masters taught Tiger how to meditate. Over the years Tiger has consulted with a Thai-born monk as well as an American Buddhist in Escondido, California, for help with his meditative techniques. His belief in the power of Buddhism was evident in the mother-of-pearl Buddha—a present from his Thai grandfather—that he kept above his bed, the gold Buddha he'd wear on a chain around his neck, and the simple white bracelet—a gift from a Buddhist monk—he wore on his wrist. Tiger would return to Thailand when he was 18 and again when he was 21, the latter visit as a conquering hero. A three-time PGA tour winner and a worldwide celebrity, he was there to play in the Asian Honda Classic in Bangkok, about 70 miles south of where his mother was raised.

More than 1,000 people gathered at the Don Muang Airport to greet Tiger after his 20-hour flight, but the next day heat exhaustion forced him quit after 13 holes of a pro-am event at the Thai Country Club. No matter: in the real tournament Tiger shot a final round 68 to win by ten strokes. "Winning period is great but to win here in Thailand is something special," he said. "This is like home to me." Afterwards Thailand's Prime Minister awarded him honorary citizenship.

Tiger has often stressed his Asian heritage above his other bloodlines, referring to his "Thainess" and calling himself "mathematically Asian." Though he does not know many Thai words beyond *kob koon* (thank you) and *mai aow* (no), it is clear he feels a deep connection to his mother's Thai culture. "He spends time paying respect to the Buddha image and asking for blessings," his mother told the *Bangkok Post* in 2000. "Buddhism helps him balance his life and not get too absorbed in illusory fame and monetary success."

Tiger is certainly not the only professional athlete to apply Zen and Buddhist principles to his life and training. Performers in all sports and, indeed, all professions, rely on meditation to strengthen and center themselves. But Tiger's golf game offers a veritable primer on Eastern thinking. Nearly every facet of his dominance can trace its roots to his Buddhist education.

This is not to say Tiger employs Buddhist thinking before every shot or every tournament. "I do not practice Buddhism on a day-to-day basis," he said in 1997. "I practice it now and then when I feel like it ... when I am weak that is usually when I practice it." Even so, every single time Tiger tees up a golf ball, he reveals positive attributes that can be traced to his Buddhist upbringing. These attributes, or virtues, are simple, straightforward, full of common sense and easy to comprehend. Each is useful in its own right and, if grasped, will lead to good things. But taken together, these attributes form a powerful prescription for living. Implementing them takes time and practice and discipline, for you are doing nothing less than gaining mastery over your mind. Buddhism does not offer its treasures to the casual observer. But those who commit themselves to making genuine changes will be richly rewarded.

It is this commitment that goes the furthest in explaining Tiger's greatness. His genius was taking not only the values he learned from his mother but also those he absorbed from his father and synthesizing them into one incredibly potent performance ethic. Add to that the nourishment of his many wonderful swing coaches, and the insight of his many golf mentors, and it is clear Tiger's mental and spiritual arsenals are more fully stocked than those of the average athlete. Yet none of this training would have mattered had Tiger not made the commitment to open up his mind and heart and welcome the wisdom of the world. None of it would matter today if Tiger was not still committed to becoming an ever-better golfer—and an ever-better man. It appears that as long as he maintains this commitment, Tiger will be able to tap into a rarified energy stream few athletes have ever been able to access. "I know there is a higher power," he has said, "and I know what I have to do to achieve what I am after."

Let us call this the Tao of Tiger—Tiger's Way. And let us call those attributes in his golf game the Tiger Virtues. Let us also look at what they have meant to Tiger, beyond his glorious golfing career; they have helped him achieve a most precious thing—love of self. Tiger has said he has never had a problem walking past a mirror and loving all that he sees. That contentment, says his father Earl, is the real reason people are drawn to Tiger—not the 340-yard drives. "People are responding to the truth," says Earl. "You take a look around the world and in all situations there are certain people to whom everyone gravitates. And when you look at who these people are you see that they are happy, at peace with themselves, able to love themselves. And other people want to be around that. What they are recognizing, whether they realize it or not, is truth."

The question, then, is this—what do each of us see when we walk past a mirror?

Come then, let us follow Tiger as he takes his journey. Let us walk 18 holes with the world's best golfer. Do not get too close, dear readers, for he is on a mission and will not be deterred. Watch from here, from behind this tree, but do not take your eyes off him, not even for a moment. The secrets of the universe are here, in that bunker, on that green. Tiger Woods can teach us things. All we have to do is watch and learn.

PART THREE:
THE TIGER VIRTUES

"GROWN MEN CAN LEARN FROM VERY LITTLE CHILDREN, FOR THE HEARTS OF CHILDREN ARE PURE."

SO SPOKE BLACK ELK, THE VISIONARY HOLY MAN of the Oglala Sioux. His wisdom runs deep and true, as anyone who has a child can attest, but a larger point may be that it is wise to look for lessons in unlikely places. Books and schools are well and good, but it is the world around us—living, breathing, tangible—that can be the most dynamic teacher. There is goodness and purity everywhere, in places we visit every day. Some insights come to us from textbooks; others arrive on gusts of wind or falling leaves.

Or even, one could say, on the pulverized solid-core ball of a pro golfer.

What follows are 18 virtues I believe are evident in the play, speech and demeanor of Tiger Woods. Some will be obvious to anyone familiar with his game. Fearlessness, for instance—it's there every time he tries a shot so risky it makes *you* sweat. Others are not as showy: Tiger's refusal to panic when his play went south in 2004 reflects the very virtuous characteristic of patience. Each of them, on its own, is a lovely and inspiring quality. Taken together, they comprise a brave and beautiful way of life.

It is worth noting that Tiger has never held up any such virtues as the right way to act or think. He has never preached or pontificated about their value to his golf. Perhaps he would even think these 18 are overblown or silly. But it is what you take from his play that matters, not what anyone tells you to take. Many lessons in life cannot be taught—they can only be learned.

These 18 virtues, then, are merely the lessons one fan learned by watching Tiger play. They are an invitation to find the wisdom that awaits you, out there in the least likely places.

WAKEFULNESS:
Live in the Moment

*"Wakefulness is the way to life. The fool sleeps as if he were already dead.
But the master is awake and he lives forever. He watches. He is clear."*
    —The Dhammapada

*"Forget the fact that I was going for three straight majors. I had to stay in
the moment. And at that moment . . . everything was one the line."*
    —Tiger Woods

IGER WOODS COULD NOT REMEMBER THE SHOT. Of
course, he'd done the same thing thousands of times—putt for
birdie. Thousands of times he had circled a green in search of slopes
and contours, contemplated the height and direction of tiny blades of
grass. Thousands of times he had crouched behind his ball, risen into
his elegant stance and begun his languid putting stroke. So many of
those times he had watched his ball roll inexorably into the cup.
Perhaps, then, it was not surprising he could not remember this shot.

Except that Tiger could not recall this shot *immediately after hitting it.* "He walked off the green and he told me, 'I don't remember
taking the putter back,'" says Earl Woods of that birdie in an event
several years ago. "He said, 'I just don't remember doing it.' He was so
in the moment, and taking the putter back was in the past.
Something he did yesterday is gone. Something he did a moment ago
is gone. Tiger's focus is always on right now."

An absolute absorption in the task at hand—this, more than anything, is the trademark of Tiger Woods. He has shown a brilliant
ability to live in the present, to shut out distractions and focus on the

essence of his chore. When we watch Tiger play golf, we are witnessing the work of a luminous mind, engaged with the world in a way few others have been able to demonstrate. "It is the most important thing on the list of his virtues: staying in the present," says David Feherty. "When you break down what Tiger does, you see that he lives each moment, whatever it is that he's doing. There is no history, there is no future, it's just, 'What am I doing right now?'"

This state of wakefulness—of being alert to the present without allowing past experiences or fears of the future to color the experience—is at the very core of Eastern philosophy. "Can you coax your mind from wandering and keep to the original oneness?" asks the *Tao Te Ching*. "Can you cleanse your inner vision until you see nothing but the light?" Such gentle exhortations to live in the present—to not just look at a flower but to really *see* the flower—can be found everywhere in Zen and Buddhist literature. Yet wakefulness is hardly an abstract philosophical notion. Just watch a child play in a sandbox to get an idea of what it means to be awake to the present. Is so much as a fraction of attention diverted to anything other than the sand, the shovel and the pale?

Better yet, watch Tiger line up a putt. Return to perhaps his most mesmerizing display of wakefulness, during the epic final round of the 2000 PGA. That year—Tiger's most magical yet—he had already won the U.S. Open and the British Open, and was now going for a third consecutive major championship. Deep in the final round he trailed a relatively unknown golfer, Bob May, by a stroke. Logic suggested that May—small in stature, slightly pudgy, resembling a good accountant more than a cutthroat pro—would crumble under the pressure of challenging the world's best player. Instead, May played bravely, beautifully—indeed, like a champion. In the fairway of the 402-yard, dogleg left 15th hole at the Valhalla Golf Club outside Louisville, Kentucky, he stood over his approach shot at 17 under par; Tiger, in the short rough, was at -16. With a creek hugging the green to the right, May had no choice but to aim away from the flag, tucked far too close to the water to serve as a reasonable target. And yet May—with four birdies in five holes on the back nine—struck a splendid 7-iron from 168 yards that finished four feet from the pin. Tiger's 8-iron from 164 yards jumped off his club and landed in a swale behind the green some four feet from the flag. Advantage: May.

Even worse for Tiger, his third shot—up and over a steep ridge with a putter—spun wildly right, away from the hole, leaving him a tricky 15-footer for par. Were Tiger to miss his long par putt and May make his short birdie chance, May would lead by a daunting three shots with only three holes to play. The very championship, it seemed, verged on the next two shots. "That was it right there," says CBS golf analyst Bobby Clampett, who called the action on the 15th green that day. "If there's a two-shot swing and May goes up by three, it doesn't look good for Tiger."

What happened next was pure theater—and became an instant part of Tiger's lore. Dressed in his traditional Sunday red, his face utterly impassive, Tiger began stalking his par putt. Hundreds of fans pressed around the green fell impossibly silent. In the eerie stillness of a late August afternoon, with the dying sun drawing a golden haze around the green, only Tiger and his caddie Steve Williams moved at all. First from behind, then from in front, then from right and left, Tiger deliberately scoped the speed and line of his putt. He appeared neither hurried nor driven by any urgency; he simply went about his task with an almost monastic discipline.

All in all, Tiger spent nearly two long minutes studying his putt—*and not once did he lift his eyes off the green, not even for an instant.* He might have glanced at his caddie, or at the crowd, or maybe at the sky to briefly relieve the tension. But no—Tiger's attention remained riveted to the green beneath his feet. Those 15 feet of manicured earth were all that mattered—all that *existed*—for Tiger in that moment. "A brass band could have marched across that green and it wouldn't have made a difference," says David Feherty, who was positioned alongside the green that afternoon. "I have seen a similar look in the eyes of Jack Nicklaus and Martina Navratilova, but neither of those had Tiger's incredible ability to be so totally alone in what they're doing." Says Clampett: "Tiger wasn't in a zone, he *was* the zone. He has what I call hyperfocus: an ability to raise your level of concentration to such a point that all you see is what you need to see. It's a real skill to develop, and Tiger has obviously attained a level of doing that that is greater than anyone else's."

There, in the dusky crucible of Valhalla, Tiger finally struck his putt. "Dig down deep," he would later say of his effort. "Concentrate, control emotions." The ball obliged its slight right-to-left break and tipped dead center in the hole. Spectators leaped to scream appreciation, but Tiger's face betrayed no trace of emotion. Bob May, apparently unnerved, spent far less time lining up his four-foot putt and, with a birdie achingly in his grasp, badly pulled the shot and missed the cup.

Both golfers walked off the 15th green with par, but the results were anything but equal. Two holes later Tiger produced another birdie to tie May, and went on to win the PGA championship in a three-hole playoff. May had played gallantly, but "there was a little bit of magic in what Tiger did that day," says Clampett. "When he desperately needs to do something, he summons that intense focus and then he goes out and does it."

Time and again, Tiger has been able to shrink his universe into a narrow increment, allowing him to engage with reality in a way few of us ever have. "Your vision will become clear only when you can look into your own heart," Carl Jung once wrote. "Who looks outside, dreams. Who looks inside, awakes."

Consider the white-knuckle final round of the 2003 President's Cup in South Africa, during which Tiger squared off against the great Ernie Els with nothing less than the Cup itself on the line. On the third hole of sudden death, in another quickly encroaching dusk, Tiger once again faced an undulating 15-footer for par. Miss it, and the United States would lose the Cup. Tiger's 11 teammates, dressed in uniform red shirts, clustered greenside to watch the world's No. 1 player prove his greatness once again—or to console him with pats on the back should he fail. "That was one of the most nerve-racking moments I've ever had in golf," Tiger said after the match. "I saw all this red and I was just trying to block that out. I just got into my little world and made the putt." Even though it only secured a tie with Els's International team, some have called it the most pressurized putt Tiger ever made.

And again, at the 2001 Masters, where a victory would give Tiger all four major pro golf championship trophies at one time—an unprecedented feat and perhaps the toughest achievement in modern sports history—Tiger put on a dazzling display of living in the present. The great Australian golfer Greg Norman once said that golf is a series of one-shot tournaments, each to be played and won before commencing with the next. Tiger's performance at the 2001 Masters proved this to be true. This time, there were no spectacular shots—none were needed—but rather a steady grind to the finish, one shot at a time. No sloppy mistakes, no mental errors, no rushed putts—just acute attention to every single swing.

So engrossed was Tiger in the task of executing each shot that, after holing out his final putt for victory on the 18th green, he did not even realize he had finished his round until a caddy congratulated him. He had just accomplished one of the great sports feats of all time—the Tiger Slam, it would be called—and yet he had no idea he had done it. "All of a sudden, I realized I had no more shots to play," he later explained. "I was done, and I had somehow come out on top." Once it sank in, Tiger's concrete composure crumbled and he welled up with emotion, hiding his face in his Nike cap.

The very idea that he would ever be distracted from his task by thoughts of the past or future is, for Tiger, simply ludicrous. "You've just got to play one shot at a time," he said in 2001. "Whatever is in the past has already been done. I'm trying to do the best that I can in the here and now, and if I started thinking about what I've done in the past, I'll forget about hitting a nice, high, shaping 2-iron up there or hitting a little low, cut 6. You can't think that way. You've got to be present when you play."

Of course, many other top athletes have been able to reach such levels of blinding focus—Michael Jordan, Joe Montana and, in golf, Jack Nicklaus and Ben Hogan come to mind. An ability to concentrate fully on demand is an indispensable skill for any professional competitor.

What makes Tiger special is the consistency of his efforts to block out distractions. "Even at the age of five, he had the ability to hit ten perfect shots in a row," says his first professional swing coach, Rudy Duran. "He'd stay in the present and hit a perfect drive, and then he'd hit a perfect second shot, and then a perfect putt, and then another perfect drive, and so on. Maybe he would miss one shot in there somewhere, but then he would hit another series of perfect shots. He is better now than he was at five, obviously, but essentially he was the same back then." Duran also makes the point that "sure, there are people on the PGA tour who can hit it as well as Tiger. But they don't seem to do it over and over again. Tiger always stays in the present and he just makes fewer mistakes."

World-class athletes tumble out of the present all the time, despite their extraordinary abilities to focus. Tiger's rival, Phil Mickelson, very nearly won the 2001 PGA but, on the par four 16th hole during the final round, he allowed himself to be yanked out of the present. Tied for the lead after holing a lovely 35-foot chip on the 15th green, but facing a brutal 50-foot putt with his third shot on 16, Mickelson could not shut out the chatter of the crowd around the green. "I've got five people in the gallery . . . telling me how slow [the green] is," he said after the round. "I tried to block it out of my mind, but it hit my subconscious. I just gave it a little bit extra." Mickelson's shot ran well past the hole and he wound up with a three-putt, falling out of the lead—and out of contention. "It's disappointing," he would say, "because I've been focusing very well all week."

Clearly, freeing one's mind of clutter and staying in the present is easier said than done, and the challenge of achieving wakefulness has fascinated all manner of thinkers, spiritualists and performance experts. Deepak Chopra's *Golf for Enlightenment* urges readers to "find the now and you'll find the shot." The great golf teacher Dr. Joseph Parent, in his excellent *Zen Golf*, breaks down the kinds of practice required to "cultivate and strengthen awareness." Performance analysts Deborah Graham and Jon Stabler refer to the desired state of alertness as "optimum arousal" in their *Eight Traits of Champion Golfers*. And David A. Cooper's wonderful *The Heart of Stillness* talks about "mastering monkey mind," the dreaded condition "when our thoughts seem to jump rapidly as though from one branch to another."

By any name, succumbing to a cluttered and undisciplined mind—recalling a past failure or thinking ahead to a future event when we should be fully focused on the present—is certainly a familiar occurrence to all of us. Indeed, how many of us can say we have truly and fully experienced more than a handful of moments in our madcap lives?

How, then, does Tiger Woods manage to make wakefulness as easy to summon as a 5-iron from his bag?

One of his great advantages is "the Zen, Buddhist and Oriental teachings his mother Tida gave him," believes Jim Huber. "It's not something that Tiger and his mother talk about, but I give her credit for instilling that peace and calm that allows Tiger to draw strength when times are difficult." Watching Tiger circle a green with deliberation and attentiveness is not unlike watching a Buddhist monk stroll around the courtyard of a monastery, focusing on the steps he is taking and nothing else. The centeredness exhibited by Tiger while reading a putt is not dissimilar to the stillness exhibited by people during meditation, the Buddhist practice of deep reflection and contemplation. Indeed, says John Anselmo, one of his early swing coaches, "Tiger can meditate himself into any frame of mind he needs. No question, the best thing about Tiger is his mind."

Tiger has admitted to the influence meditation exerts on his golf and on his life. "What techniques do you use to keep focused, be spiritually at ease and consistently perform the way you do?" one fan asked in a *Golf Digest* e-mail exchange with Tiger. His reply: "It has a lot to do with my upbringing. My mother introduced me to meditation because of her Buddhist background . . . I don't meditate nearly as much as I used to, but I've learned the techniques. . . . I now do it daily without even thinking about it."

Some have suggested that through his work with sports psychologist Jay Brunza, Tiger has learned to slip into a deep meditative trance while playing, allowing him to concentrate at superhuman levels. "Does he go into a trance? Well, we don't know," says Anselmo. "I know Brunza really helped him in this area. But Tiger was already doing all of this—controlling himself, balancing things—when he was a kid."

The furthest Tiger has gone in discussing his specific pre-shot regimen—the precise way he slips into a state of hyperfocus—is to say, in his book *How I Play Golf*, that "before an important shot, I relax myself by taking a long, deep breath"—a cleansing breath. Says Tiger's father, Earl, "Learning how to live in the moment takes not just practice, but commitment. You have to really decide to live your life for right now."

True wakefulness, then, is not something a single chapter, or even an entire volume, can bring about. It is a discipline that requires a far lengthier and more demanding commitment than merely reading a book. At the same time, it is impossible to overstate the importance of wakefulness in improving performance and life itself. Without it, we can never hope to tap our full potential. "What Tiger is demonstrating is the power of human energy when it is properly managed," says Dr. Jim Loehr. "When you see someone recruit the energy of the body and of the heart and of the mind and of the spirit and get them all in alignment, that is when you see people go way outside the box and do something they have never been able to do before. And Tiger Woods is truly the embodiment of that. When you watch him, he is one hundred percent there, very present and in the moment. And that is what produces the extraordinary."

Begin, then, by watching Tiger Woods play golf. Notice the precision of his movements, the intensity in his narrowed eyes, the sureness of his swings, the overall poise and grace. Heed his unchanging pre-shot rituals, his authority around the greens. Pay attention to the way he carries himself—deliberate, dignified, in control. Then notice how, with few exceptions, *he is always this way.*

The people of Florence in 13th century Italy would hurry to the street just to watch Leonardo da Vinci stroll by, so evocative of strength and purpose was his gait. Tiger, too, seems able to entrance fans with his every movement: win or lose, he routinely draws the biggest galleries at any event. "Follow then the shining ones," *The Dhammapada* tells us, "the wise, the awakened, the loving, for they know how to work and forbear."

Not convinced that Tiger is one of the shining ones? That he is more alert to the moment or attuned to reality than the average fellow? Consider this: a while back, Nike Golf sent Tiger five prototype drivers to try out. He practiced with each and revealed that his favorite was the heaviest. Nike's club makers were baffled, since they believed all five clubs weighed the same. They put the clubs on the scales and, sure enough, discovered that Tiger's favorite was indeed heavier.

By less than an ounce.

HUMILITY:
Don't Boast, Be Gracious

"Humility is the root of greatness. Those in high places do well to think of themselves as powerless, small and unworthy. Attain honor without being honored. Don't shine like jade, or chime like bells."
—*The Tao Te Ching*

"I've worked really hard. And again, I've been really lucky, too. I've had some good breaks and some good things in my life go the right way. And it could have easily gone the other way."
—*Tiger Woods*

TIGER WOODS HAD JUST WON the 2001 Memorial Tournament. He had just walloped runners-up Paul Azinger and Sergio Garcia by no less than seven strokes. He had just shot four straight rounds in the 60s, the only golfer in the event to do so at the challenging Muirfield Village Golf Club in Dublin, Ohio. He had just won the tournament—created and hosted by his idol, Jack Nicklaus—for an unprecedented third year in a row.

What's more, when he won the 2001 Memorial he already had, sitting on his mantle at home, the trophies from all four professional major championships—the 2000 U.S. Open, the 2000 British Open, the 2000 PGA and the 2001 Masters—the first time in golf history that all four titles belonged to one man at one time. Tiger Woods had just solidified his place as the most dominant, proficient and thoroughly exceptional golfer of his, and perhaps any other, generation. And he had done so at the age of 26. What, then, did he have to say for himself as he walked off the 18th green at Muirfield and shook hands with Jack Nicklaus? Three words.

"I got lucky."

Huh? Lucky? Here's the very best golfer in the world, at the very height of his powers, attributing one of his more dominant victories to luck? You win the Memorial by one or two shots, maybe it's luck. But seven strokes? And three years in a row? And four straight majors? Surely, Tiger was being disingenuous, falsely modest—surely his superior skills, unmatched discipline and ability to intimidate had far, far more to do with his Memorial win than mere good fortune. So what exactly did Tiger mean when he said, "I got lucky?"

In fact, Tiger was demonstrating one of his more consistent character virtues—humility. To have a modest sense of one's significance, even when one is as significant a figure as Tiger Woods, does not mean you are being insincere. In Tiger's case, he is merely adhering to his Buddhist beliefs. "A man who boasts of his achievements has no merit," says the *Tao Te Ching.* "A man who brags will not endure. To a person of Tao, these things are excess food and superfluous behavior. Because nothing good can come of them, he doesn't indulge in them."

At a time when so many superstar athletes indulge in superfluous behavior—trash-talking, crass showmanship, obscene antics—Tiger's consistent humility is downright radical. "There is no cockiness there at all," says Jim Huber. "He believes in himself, but at the same time he respects the game of golf so much, he respects its principles and everything it stands for. I don't think you will ever catch him doing something that would disgrace himself or the game."

It is true that the sport of golf is uniquely devoid of boorish characters—even its occasional quacks and eccentrics are, by and large, mindful of the game's traditions and rituals. The very essence of golf has to do with honor, respect, civility, and, indeed, humility. It is unlikely you will ever catch any professional golfer vowing to squash someone like a bug or strutting after an eagle putt. In this sense, Tiger's inherent modesty is merely par for the course. But when you consider how much responsibility he carries as a role model—and how easy it would be for him to have a swelled head—it becomes easier to appreciate just how consistent and special his conduct is. "My kids now, they idolize Tiger; gosh, all kids do," says his former coach John Anselmo. "Growing up a lot of the kids he played against didn't much care for Tiger because he was too good and he was winning everything. The same was true when he turned pro. So Tiger has had to prove himself not only as a golfer but also as an individual—as a good person. And he has done a wonderful job with that."

Tiger's good friend Charles Barkley, the former NBA superstar known for being brash and opinionated, once called Tiger "the most humble celebrity I've ever met in my life. . . . If I had his golf swing and his money, oh, I'd walk around with a bullhorn letting people known when I was coming around." Not Tiger. He turns down every chance to toot his own horn. Asked if he was the most dominant athlete in the world—at a time when he very clearly was—Tiger replied, "I think if someone is going to be considered that, I think they would have to be a little bit bigger than me. I'm just a six-foot guy chasing a little white ball."

Ironically, early in his professional career Tiger delivered the closest thing to trash-talking golf has ever seen. "He would talk about how he had won this or that tournament with his 'b' or his 'c' game, not his 'a' game," says Gary McCord, describing a practice that irritated some veteran players Tiger was trouncing. "He wasn't being flip or anything, he was just a 21-year-old kid sticking his chest out. But he learned pretty quick not to do that anymore. *Real quick*." Today, Tiger expertly juggles the healthy ego needed to pull off dangerous shots and a seemingly ego-free attitude about his accomplishments. "You need an extremely high opinion of yourself to perform at the level Tiger does," says David Feherty, "and that is why some people make a real mess of winning by saying the wrong things. But Tiger understands the whole picture, including what people are expecting of him. He knows how he wants to be perceived and he does what he needs to do."

Just listen to Tiger answering a question about his marvelous play in 2001: "I've been very fortunate to have won the tournaments that I've won." And again, later that year: "I've been blessed to play the way that I have the past few years. On top of that, I've had a lot of good breaks." And again in 2003: "The times that I have won I've had some great breaks go my way—shots hit in trees spit out back in fairways, a bad shot that gets a good bounce and allows you to make par. You need to have those types of breaks." Asked about his gutsy win over Bob May at the 2000 PGA, he said, "I was fortunate enough to make a big putt on 15 for par, and Bob missed a reasonably short putt for birdie, which was big for me. . . . I was fortunate enough to make one more [birdie] than he did." Tiger even deflected credit for his four major victories in a row, a feat some have called the greatest in sports history. "To have it happen four straight times, that's awfully nice," he said. "Some of the golf gods are looking down on me the right way." He did not win the four straight majors—they just happened. To hear Tiger tell it, he was just along for the ride.

In Buddhist terms this is known as Right Speech. "One avoids vain talk and abstains from it," explains the *Anguttara Nikaya*, a collection of Buddhist wisdom. "One speaks at the right time, in accordance with facts, speaks what is useful, speaks of the law and the discipline; one's speech is like a treasure, uttered at the right moment, accompanied by understanding, moderate, and full of sense. This is called Right Speech."

But does Tiger really owe his success to the occasional lucky bounce? At the 2000 British Open, Tiger somehow avoided putting a single ball into any of St. Andrew's 112 bunkers for four straight rounds, an absolutely inexplicable feat. "I'm surprised at some of the fortunate breaks I've gotten," Tiger said afterwards. "I hit some bad shots that ended up all right . . . you need some lucky bounces." But even Jack Nicklaus was skeptical. "You don't get lucky bounces," he said, "for four straight days."

Tiger knows very well that his skills play more of a role in his success than lucky breaks. But it is Right Speech to acknowledge the role of the fortunate first and foremost. Besides, Tiger's humility runs much deeper than appreciating a good hop. Start with the genetic bounty of his granite physique. "I've been blessed with the physical ability to execute whatever shot my mind dictates," Tiger wrote in his book.

Then came his fortuitous schooling in Buddhism, coupled with his father's determination to instill rock-solid values in his son. "I taught him not to develop an attitude that he is better than anyone else," says Earl. "I tried to make him understand how other people felt and what impact he would have on others. He learned that you are as you are perceived, and for that reason it is important to be humble."

As a freshman in high school, Tiger instantly became his team's leader, something that might have caused problems had he approached it the wrong way. But "Tiger was never overbearing about it," says his high school coach Don Crosby. "He never got mad at the kids when they did something he thought was wrong; that just wasn't who he was. What you see is what you get with Tiger. There was never anything phony about it."

In college, Tiger was again the star of his team, and yet "was not the slightest bit arrogant," says his Stanford coach Wally Goodwin. "I've had all kinds of kids, and some kids, after a couple of years, they become so arrogant it's like they feel the world owes them something. But Tiger never asked for anything, ever." Despite comprising one of the greatest collegiate teams of all time, Tiger and his Stanford teammates "never lorded it over anyone," says Goodwin. "They were very generous to their opponents and very gracious in defeat and they always had a good thought at the end of tournaments. When they won they didn't jump in a lake or anything. They were remarkable guys."

On top of Tiger's reflexive humility, he possesses the understanding that golf is, more than most sports, a game of breaks and bounces. "In golf, you're always lucky to win, even at Tiger's level of ability," says Goodwin, who recalls coming across another great young golfer two decades before Tiger Woods. "A wonderful kid named Bobby Clampett, who people called the next Jack Nicklaus," says Goodwin. "Well, one time, Bobby was going to play some tournament, and I said, 'Good luck.' And his father said, 'Don't you ever wish him luck again. It has nothing to do with luck.' And I thought to myself, 'It's practically *all* about luck.' A lot of guys can get the ball to the hole. But you need the lucky bounce or break to win. And if you don't think luck is involved, you're heading for the psychiatrist's office." Clampett never achieved the success predicted for him, in part, no doubt, because of some bad breaks along the way.

Tiger, then, was lucky to have been raised by parents who value humility and weaned on a sport that does the same. "The game of golf teaches people at a very young age to be gracious in victory and gracious in defeat," says Roger Maltbie. "You look at Jack Nicklaus, a guy who absolutely hated to lose, and he was the first guy to stick out his hand and congratulate the winner. The more humble you are and the more appreciative you are of the things that went your way, the greater a winner that makes you."

Yet no matter how ingrained it is in Tiger to be modest, humility is, like his other virtues, something that needs to be practiced. Think it's easy being humble when you know your talents and intellect are superior? Benjamin Franklin didn't. "There is perhaps no one of our natural passions so hard to subdue as pride," the great Franklin once wrote. "Disguise it, struggle with it, beat it down, stifle it, mortify it as much as one pleases, it is still alive and will every now and then peep out and show itself." Even if he were to succeed in tamping down his pride, admitted Franklin, "I would probably be proud of my humility."

Tiger, too, has wrestled with pride, a struggle manifest in that most human of failings—making excuses. For most of his career, Tiger did not come within a two-iron of an excuse. "He always fessed up to everything and he had an easy manner about it when he did not play well," says David Feherty. But in the past two years—during the second of his two so-called slumps—he has occasionally blamed different factors for his poor play.

At the 2003 Masters, he made a rare mental mistake by pulling his driver on the third tee, some 330 yards from the green, instead of playing it safe with an iron. His tee shot screeched into the woods and led to a double bogey, derailing his chance of winning a third straight Masters. Later, he appeared to blame caddy Steve Williams for talking him into using the driver. "I wanted to hit an iron, but Steve said it was a better play from down below," Tiger said. "It was a bad decision." (To his credit, he quickly added, "Ultimately, it's the player's call").

Tiger has also complained about sticky grass, hard greens and overly penal layouts—carps that would never have slipped through his lips in his heyday. One might wonder why it's okay to credit wins to lucky breaks but not to blame losses on bad bounces? As the *Tao Te Ching* warns, "A man who justifies his actions is not respected."

But, hey, Tiger is human, and now and then he's going to make mistakes. Because of his inherent humility, though, he is bound to make far fewer of them than your average superstar. "He has always been that way," says his dad. "He was never cocky, never had a mean streak. Believe it or not, when Tiger was young, I never once had to punish him for anything."

No time outs, groundings or supperless nights in 18 years? Now *that's* an impressive streak.

PREPARATION:
Good Habits, Good Life

"Do not neglect your own duty for another, however great. Know your own duty and perform it."
—The Dhammapada

"Control yourself and you control your destiny."
—Tiger Woods

DID YOU HEAR THE ONE ABOUT THE GOLFER and the basketball player who walk into a bar in Hawaii? The golfer, Rich Beem, had impressively held off a hard-charging Tiger Woods to win the 2002 PGA, but midway through their current event—the 2002 Grand Slam—Tiger was utterly trouncing him. Despite his big win, Beem sensed he wasn't yet in a league with Tiger. So there in the bar, with midnight approaching, he turned to the retired basketball star—Charles Barkley, now a TNT commentator—and asked, "You're good friends with Tiger. Tell me, how do I beat this guy?" Barkley looked at his wristwatch. "I'll tell you one thing," he said. "Tiger has been in bed for two hours now, so you're not going to beat him in here."

Okay, so maybe Tiger Woods will never be the life of the party; heck, he probably won't even be at the party. But he is a shining example of the virtue of being prepared. Tiger is intent on doing anything and everything it takes to put himself in the absolute best position to win—not occasionally or even most of the time, but every time. He understands the bulk of his work needs to be done long before he sets foot on a golf course, and he appreciates the huge sacrifices required to set the stage for success. To leave any avenue of improvement unexplored or overlook any detail large or small is to cede an advantage to your opponent and turn the outcome much more into a matter of chance. This, Tiger Woods is unwilling to do. More than most athletes, he covers *all* the bases. "The attention to detail is incredible," says David Feherty. "Tiger takes care of everything, absolutely everything. You get the impression that it doesn't really matter what he chose to do, he could make a living doing it. No, he could make a *fortune* doing it."

Every top athlete devotes countless hours to preparing for performance—to creating the conditions needed for giving their best effort. But the extent of Tiger's devotion quite simply revolutionized his sport. From the very beginning, Tiger's game plan was to be the best prepared, best conditioned and most disciplined competitor in any field—to complement his amazing talent with unrivaled dedication. His mind-blowing success—winning seven of 11 majors and nearly 40 percent of his starts at one point—becomes much easier to comprehend given this simple formula: the most talented golfer in the game routinely outworked and out-prepared everyone else. "With Tiger, it's all about preparation," continues Feherty. "When he gets to the golf course, he's already flipped that switch. Before he walks out there, he's made a conscious decision that this is who he is, this is what he wants to be and this is what it takes to get there. He has decided what he wants his world to look like, and he makes sure he is always in control."

Tiger's preparedness extends well beyond the endless hours he spends on the practice range refining and improving his swing. What he eats, how much he sleeps, his physical condition, even what he wears—all these factors and many more are part of what Tiger considers his good duty. The discipline needed to precisely calibrate these elements and bring them up to Tiger's high standards is daunting, but even more so in Tiger's case because of the extraordinary demands on his time. He has had to create and defend various rituals that insure he will always be able to prepare in the manner he chooses. It is not an easy thing to do, but it is not supposed to be. In Buddhist teachings, preparedness is a way in which you can gain mastery and set yourself apart from others. "To straighten the crooked, you must first do a harder thing—straighten yourself," instructs *The Dhammapada*. "You are your only master. Who else? Subdue yourself and discover your master."

His Buddhist upbringing, together with his father's beliefs in the natural flow of the universe, turned preparedness into a reflex for Tiger. "There are things in your life that you don't feel are quite right, so you change them," he once explained. "And you've got to tweak them every day, because it's very easy to get out of balance and not have everything exactly as you would like to have it. It could be that you're sleeping too much or not sleeping enough. Or you're not eating enough or eating too much. You've just got to keep the right balance."

Up and down the line, Tiger zealously guards the conditions needed to maximize his talents. "Everything around him, everything he does, the people he associates with—everything has to be within his parameters," says Gary McCord. "To get to the level that Tiger has, you have to live an impeccable life." McCord's notion of an impeccable life is not unlike what the scholar Joseph Campbell had in mind when he spoke of the heroic impulse in each of us. "One way or another, we all have to find what best fosters the flowering of our humanity in this contemporary life, and dedicate ourselves to that," he said in *The Power of Myth*. "The world is full of people who have stopped listening to themselves or have listened only to their neighbors to learn what they ought to do, how they ought to behave and what the values are that they should be living for."

Tiger's humanity is flowering just fine, thank you. To keep it that way, he makes sure he gets his usual five or six hours of sleep a night in weeks when he's competing. Considering how he likes to wake up with the roosters for pre-dawn jogs and early practice rounds, getting those precious few hours of sleep means no late nights on the town. "Tiger didn't waste any time partying, none at all," remembers his high school coach Don Crosby. "He always knew what he needed to do to get a good education and play good golf."

That hasn't changed much since Tiger turned pro, but the same cannot be said of his physique. The Tiger who played his first pro event in 1996—6'2", 155 pounds, on the scrawny side—is long gone. In his place, an Adonis, packed with 25 extra pounds of muscle. "Bumping into him is like bumping into a refrigerator," says Jim

Huber. "He is just so solid, a rock. If you saw him in the locker room with his shirt off, you would think he was a boxer. I mean, he works out two or three times a day, he runs, he swims, he lifts weights. He is a specimen."

It is by now a central plank of his legend that Tiger's devotion to physical conditioning not only transformed him into the most athletic golfer ever, but also transformed the sport of golf itself. "For a long time, it was thought you didn't need a lot of physicality to hit a golf ball," says Dr. Jim Loehr. "What Tiger found and demonstrated conclusively is that even if you don't run ten miles while playing a round of golf, having a lot of energy is a very important part of being successful in pressure situations in golf."

Much has been made of Tiger's secret workout routines, but the specifics of his regimen matter less than its consistency. In his book *How I Play Golf* Tiger devotes a chapter to the importance of getting stronger and reveals the basics of his workouts. There is nothing radical there, except in the obvious intensity of his approach. "Any workout routine must be regimented and consistent," he writes. "It requires a real commitment to building a powerful body."

Because Tiger's ferocious swing contorts his body into frightening positions, the time he spends stretching is particularly crucial. Likewise, his ability to stay focused for four or five hours during rounds depends on never becoming physically fatigued, and so Tiger—a cross-country runner when he was younger—likes to run in all types of weather and makes sure he scales a hill or two during his jogs. Working with free weights—long thought to be detrimental for golfers who needed to be lithe, not bulky—has contributed to Tiger's power off the tee (among other areas, he pays attention to building up his lats, shoulders, chest, triceps, wrists and stomach). They key to his workouts is that Tiger attacks them as if he were a linebacker for the Green Bay Packers. "Tiger could start in the NFL tomorrow," says David Feherty. "People who have worked with him and trained him have told me, 'Tiger is the best all-around athlete on the planet right now.' He just doesn't get to show it."

Again, the point is not what Tiger does in his workouts, it is that he rarely misses one. You may not ever be able to do 600 to 1000 sit-ups a day, as Tiger has been known to do, but you can faithfully stick to your plan, as Tiger always does. When he's on the road, he'll find a local gym or someone who owns free weights. Even the absence of equipment is no excuse: one of Tiger's hand-strengthening exercises is scrunching up pages of a newspaper one at a time. "Sounds easy," he has said, "but it isn't."

Tiger's devotion to training—the way in which he never neglects his own duty—has had more of an impact on his sport than the actions of any other athlete in recent memory. Thanks to Tiger, the modern golfer is no longer slump-shouldered or pot-bellied. Today's typical pro golfer, while perhaps not as thick or chiseled as Tiger, is far more athletic than just a few years ago. "The PGA always had an exercise trailer on site, but before Tiger you could have thrown a bomb in there and not hurt anyone," says Jim Loehr. "Now they have two trailers and you have to schedule a time to get in there."

Of course, Tiger's athleticism depends on more than running and lifting-weights; his preparedness also includes acute attention to nutrition. A former fast-food junkie fond of McDonalds hamburgers and Taco Bell, Tiger revamped his diet not long after turning pro. The focus is now on low-fat foods—fruits, vegetables, chicken and fish—and away from pizza, fried foods and sweets. While he loves strawberry milkshakes and will indulge in the occasional beer or burger, Tiger generally sticks to his healthy menu regardless of circumstances. For instance, when he is in a foreign country—which, in his case, is just about every other week—Tiger only rarely samples the local cuisine. Not because he doesn't want to, but because he knows it is safer to stick with familiar foods. "If I get sick," he once explained, "I can't play." Creating the conditions for optimal performance takes precedence over everything else. "Live purely," *The Dhammapada* advises. "Do your work, with mastery. Like the moon, come out from behind the clouds! Shine."

One way Tiger insures the integrity of his important rituals is by being just as attentive to the less important ones. For instance, he is meticulous about his attire. Early in his pro career, Tiger looked like any 20-year-old. At his pro debut in the 1996 Greater Milwaukee Open, his black Nike shirt was a little baggy and only half tucked-in. The top button was casually open. Like his slender build, that look would quickly be replaced. Along with his newly-bulked up body, Tiger introduced a new fashion sense: crisp, clean, neat, perfect. Today, "the collar is always buttoned, the shirt is always tucked in, the pants are always creased," says Gary McCord. "And I mean always. You'll never catch Tiger with his shirttail out. This guy would not have fit in in the grunge scene in Seattle."

Some might say Tiger is a full-blown neatnick: he insists on ironing his own clothing every morning. "Even if it's dry-cleaned," he admitted, "I'll iron it just a little bit, all the little creases." And he makes his bed every day, even when he's in a hotel. Not meticulous enough for you? Well, what about being fully focused and prepared just to go shopping? "I do it very efficiently," Tiger has said. "No wasted movement." Even the way Tiger folds his scorecard—precisely, attentively, the same way every time—reflects a high level of care and commitment.

But, it is reasonable to ask, does it really matter how Tiger folds his scorecard? Can something so insignificant have any bearing on how he plays? "The precision that you show in cleaning out your glove compartment or driving your car is connected to everything else you do," says Dr. Jim Loehr. "You are learning how to approach tasks that *are* important. You are learning how to summon a sense of commitment and excellence, so that you always do the best that you can. Because what you are really doing is mobilizing for the big moment. When something that really matters comes along, you will be ready to fully engage in doing it."

No stone unturned, no task undone, no detail overlooked. Even as a lad, Tiger liked his golf balls to be spotless. "He wasn't unique in that he cleaned them, but what was funny is that he had to stand on top of the spike cleaners to reach the ball washer," remembers Rudy Duran. "I would see him clinging to the very top of the washer just to not fall off. But still he always cleaned his golf balls. Even when he was five or six, hanging around with him was like hanging around with another golf pro."

His high school coach Don Crosby remembers a tournament on Vancouver Island, in which Tiger faced a tricky third shot on the long par five 18th hole. One of the hundreds of spectators gathered to watch Tiger play took note of the lie—15 feet off the green, in three-inch rough, on a steep slope—and said aloud, "He'll be lucky to get this on the green." Don Crosby heard this and smiled. "Normally I don't say anything but this time I told the guy, 'You'll be amazed how close he gets this.' So Tiger hits the ball and it takes two bounces and goes in the hole."

What Crosby knew—and the spectator didn't—was that in an earlier practice session Tiger had gone out of his way to drop several balls in a similar spot near the 18th green so he could practice the difficult flop shot. "He figured his second shot might end up there so he practiced the shot, trying to get it close," says Crosby. "The closest one he got in practice was four or five feet. But the point is, when the real shot came up, he was ready. He was prepared."

At Stanford, Tiger was similarly devoted to being prepared, despite having to juggle golf and a full course load. "One time, we got back from a tournament in Tennessee late on a Saturday night," says his coach Wally Goodwin. "It was the end of the year and everyone had exams and term papers. Well, two days later Tiger walks into my office and he's pale—completely white. He says, 'I haven't slept since we got from Chattanooga, I took my exams and did my two term papers and I'm on my way home—see you in the fall.' He would just sit down and do what had to be done. He wouldn't sit around and talk to a girl for an hour, he would take care of business first."

As with many things, Tiger gives much of the credit for this virtue to his parents. His mother harped on the importance of discipline while his father drilled him in the ways he could improve his sense of self. "A lot of people don't know where to start making changes and wind up muddling through life bumbling from one thing to another," says Earl Woods, who collected his thoughts on self-improvement in his books *Training a Tiger* and *Playing Through*. "All you have to do is start with something simple. Always put your clothes on a hanger. Always be on time. Nobody will know something is different except for you. But you will notice the change in yourself. Next, devote thirty more minutes a night to studying. Now things are starting to accumulate. Now your grades improve. And your perception of self becomes, 'Hey, I can do this.'"

And so it becomes clear: by strenuously preparing for his tasks, by zealously guarding his rituals, by doing both the big and the little things right, Tiger controls himself and, thus, controls his destiny. This, the Buddha would say, is Right Action. "If you do what is good, keep repeating it and take pleasure in making it a habit," says *The Dhammapada*. "A good habit will cause nothing but joy."

So, did you hear the one about the golfer who irons his dry-cleaned shirts and goes around scrunching up newspapers and folds his scorecard like Felix Ungar and likes to go running in the rain? Not a very funny one, is it?

POSITIVE THINKING:
Don't Be Too Self-Critical

"Concentrate on power and you'll experience power. Concentrate on loss and you'll experience loss."
—*The Tao Te Ching*

"I believe in every shot I hit that I can pull it off. It's just, I guess, my mindset. I've always believed that."
—*Tiger Woods*

I T WAS THE NO. 1 LOCKER ROOM TOPIC in golf: what's wrong with Tiger Woods? After what seemed like every round he played in late 2003 and most of 2004, reporters would ask Tiger why he wasn't winning, how could he fix it, when would his slump end? Tiger would have none of it, refusing to even use the dreaded "s" word to describe his play. At one stop, an exasperated reporter finally asked, "Have you ever been in a slump in your life?" Tiger did not hesitate. "No," he replied, ""I've been playing pretty good ever since I came out of the womb."

False bravado? Deep denial? Actually, Tiger's statement was only a slight exaggeration. His very first swing, at all of ten months old, was so technically impressive "my jaw dropped and I almost fell out of my chair," says his father Earl. Ever since then, Tiger has pretty much played dazzling golf at every level, including—and most dramatically—on the pro tour. The slump that reporters talk about—no major wins in more than two years, only a handful of victories in regular events, plenty of bad rounds, missed chances and wayward drives—was, by all objective measures, only a slump when compared to Tiger's performance in seasons past. After all, he made the cut in every event he entered and had a chance to win many of them. "From a talent point of view, it's not a slump at all," says David Feherty. "If you look at the history of the game, no one, not even Jack Nicklaus, has been able to keep up the kind of standard that Tiger set. He raised the bar so high that it's completely impossible for him to keep going over it. But that doesn't mean the quality of his shots or anything that he does is any less remarkable."

Still, there can be no doubt that Tiger's overall play was considerably less stellar in 2003 and 2004 than it was in years past. Nor can Tiger deny that his driving, in particular, was far less proficient than in his heyday; in some events, he hit only three or four fairways out of 14, a poor performance by any standard. At the end of 2004 he dropped from No. 1 to No. 3 in the world rankings. So why does Tiger resist the easy categorization of his recent play as a slump? Why challenge the popular notion that his game is going downhill? The reason is simple: Tiger believes in the extraordinary power of positive thoughts and words. That is why he insists on his own analysis of his game: not that he is playing poorly, but that his play is *improving*.

Sound like semantic nitpicking? Perhaps, but it's also consistent with the teachings of the Buddha. "Our life is shaped by our mind; we become what we think," the very first lines of the *The Dhammapada* explain. "Suffering follows an evil thought as the wheels of a cart follow the oxen that draw it."

This is why Tiger toes the line when it comes to denying a slump: there is no upside in dissecting the negative aspects of his game with the press. Quite the contrary: were Tiger to continually discuss his "slump," isn't it likely those negative thoughts would crowd out the positive ones in his mind? This is not to say that Tiger refuses to examine the flaws in his game. In fact, he is as known for relentlessly scrutinizing the most minute aspects of his swing—and for having the nerve to apply drastic changes to it, if he feels they are needed. But part of Tiger's mental toughness is that he couches these changes not in negative terms—something is bad, it must be fixed—but in positive ones: there is room for improvement, I can become better. "Harsh self-criticism is a set-up for failure and misery," Chungliang Al Huang and Jerry Lynch point out in their excellent

Thinking Body, Dancing Mind. "The words you choose to cultivate in yourself as an athlete will determine your identity and beliefs about yourself."

It's not surprising that Tiger will not allow the words and labels that other people use influence how he perceives his own play. "I don't know whether it's Zen or Taoism or something in between, but Tiger is remarkably easy on himself in public and extremely hard on himself in private," says David Feherty. "The thing is, there has never been another golfer who has been as scrutinized as Tiger—every move he makes, every word he says. Everyone wants a piece of him, wants to dissect everything he says and does. And so everything Tiger says is carefully worded. That's the way he keeps control over his world."

Tiger's positive thinking manifests itself in both his thoughts during a round and in the words he speaks afterwards. On the course, he has few rivals when it comes to strength of mind. In his book, Tiger describes one of his more amazing shots: his approach to the 18th green in the final round of the 2001 Bay Hill Invitational. Needing a birdie to hold off Phil Mickelson, Tiger yanked his tee shot left and hit a spectator, which luckily kept it from going out of bounds. Despite playing poorly most of the day, he knew he could still gut out one more birdie and get the win. But his ball was sitting 192 yards from the pin on a slick, trampled piece of turf left of a cart path. Tiger would have to cleanly hit the ball and carry it over water to reach the flag, tucked back right. Even a slight miss would put the ball in the pond. His previous bad shots during the round could have caused self-doubt to creep in. But, as Tiger explained in his book, "Never did I let a negative thought enter my head." He struck the ball perfectly and landed it 15 feet from the hole. Tiger canned the birdie putt and won by a stroke. "If you think you can't do something," he would say, "chances are you won't be able to."

Is it possible to be mentally tough enough to banish all negative thoughts precisely when you need to most? After all, just *thinking* about blocking bad thoughts can bring them front and center. "Do not imagine the Mona Lisa with a mustache!" instructs Michael J. Geld in *How to Think Like Leonardo da Vinci*, as to way to illustrate how quickly the mind turns thoughts into mental images (admit it: you pictured a mustachied Mona, didn't you?). As da Vinci himself put it, "the thing imagined moves the sense." Any good golf instructor knows one of the most common mistakes amateur players make is allowing negative thoughts to govern their actions. Faced with a great big lake to carry, the amateur tells himself, "Don't go into the water." The mind then produces an image of the ball getting wet. "This is a lesson that I've taught to many golfers," says Earl Woods. "The subconscious mind only hears the active part of your thought, so that it comes through as, 'Go in the water,'" not 'Don't go in the water.' That's the way it works. But it's also very easily to replace negative thoughts with positive thoughts, because they are just thoughts."

What Earl advises, and professional players know to do, is to feed the subconscious mind positive imagery. Facing the same obstacle, the pro player tells himself, "I want my ball to land five feet from the flag." They do not allow the mind to process any information about the hazard—it's like it doesn't even exist. Remember what the Buddha said: "Our life is shaped by our mind; we become what we think."

Consider, for example, the case of the great Minnesota Twins pitcher Jack Morris, who in 1991 took the mound for what some have called the best World Series Game 7 ever. He pitched 10 scoreless innings against the brilliant Atlanta Braves under unbelievable pressure, refusing to yield a run until his team scored to win the game in the final inning. The key to his gutsy, magical performance? Positive thinking. "I never had as much will to win a game as I did during that day," Morris would later say. "I was in trouble many times during that game, but didn't realize it because I never once had a negative thought."

In golf, Jack Nicklaus didn't have a steel-trap mind—he had a Brinks vault brain. His incredible drive and desire, uncorrupted by negative thoughts, funneled into a fierce will he could impose at opportune times. Much more often than not, Nicklaus hit the big shots and the long putts just when he needed to—and, more often than not, his opponents failed to. Nicklaus's power of positive thinking was so intimidating to his rivals that he came to count on it as a secret weapon. "Were you always confident you could beat the other guys all the time," Jim McKay once asked him. "No," replied Nicklaus, "but the other guys were."

Tiger is Jack's successor in the strength of mind department. He, too, counts on being mentally tougher than anyone else in the field. "I've felt that I've always had a mental edge over a lot of my opponents," he has said. "My mind won me a lot of tournaments." And the bigger the stakes, the more Tiger can count on that edge. "I've always felt that majors are probably going to be the easier tournaments to win," he said in 2003. "A lot of guys will eliminate themselves from the tournament mentally."

In other words, some athletes allow negative thoughts about past performances to dent their confidence, inhibit their actions and prevent them from raising their games when they need to. "There are a couple of golfers I won't name who can start getting down on themselves during rounds, and that leads to their downfalls," says Jim Huber. "But not Tiger. I remember one time a reporter asked him if he let a first round match play loss the year before enter his mind when he was playing. And Tiger just looked at him and said, 'No.' It's just not something he would allow to happen. Tiger is a very positive kid."

Still, nobody can block out all negative thoughts all the time—not even Tiger. "It's not that he was always thinking positively," says his Stanford coach Wally Goodwin. "It's that he was able to do it more than anyone else." Every once in a while, "Tiger will come up to me during a round and say, under his breath, 'God, I really suck today,'" says David Feherty. "But that's just him being angry with himself for a bad shot. When the round is over, you know he's not going to go with that as his sound bite."

That's because Tiger does not stop thinking positively once his round is over. Even when he is way behind the leaders, Tiger refuses to count himself out, a trait that tends to irritate sports journalists. Trailing by nine strokes after three rounds of the 2004 U.S. Open, Tiger told reporters, "If the wind blows and I play a great round, I can still win." *Sports Illustrated's* Rick Reilly later responded, "Yes, if the wind blows the players' hotel over and everybody else is trapped until Monday, *then* he'd win."

Likewise, when Tiger has difficult rounds, he doesn't talk about the bad shots but instead about what went right. Some might say he is merely putting the best spin he can on terrible play—in other words, being disingenuous. But in almost every round he plays, Tiger finds something positive to focus on, and uses it as the prism through which he views his efforts. To do otherwise is to risk allowing the negative terminology used by reporters to take root in his mind. However much he is prodded, Tiger simply refuses to beat himself up. When asked repeatedly about how frustrating it was to play poorly in the third round of the 2001 U.S. Open, Tiger replied, "I don't know what you guys were watching on TV, but I felt like I really played good. . . . I hit a lot of good putts today that just didn't go in. But I rolled the ball beautifully, I can't complain." Asked what went wrong after a disappointing final round in the 2001 British Open, Tiger answered, "Not a whole lot, actually. I drove the ball beautifully; I drove it on a string. . . . I hit such a beautiful putt there [on seven]; it just didn't go in."

Even when David Feherty asked him to categorize his 2004 season—described by everyone else as one long disappointment—Tiger refused to play along. "It's been both successful," he said, "and frustrating." Notice the positive thought came first. As Eleanor Roosevelt once said, "No one can make you feel inferior without your consent."

Which is not to say that they can't try. One of Tiger's favorite replies to questions about his so-called slump is to say, over and over, "I'm close." In the summer of 2004, this proved too much for some commentators to bear. During the U.S. Open, Tiger's former swing coach, Butch Harmon—whose dismissal coincided with the dip in Tiger's fortunes—took a swipe at his former pupil while working as a TV analyst. "He is not working on the right things in his golf swing in my opinion," Harmon said. "Obviously Tiger thinks he is. [But] for him to stand there in every one of his interviews and say, 'I'm close, I feel good about what I'm doing,' I think it might be a little denial."

Once again, Tiger did not take the bait. "Obviously [Harmon] doesn't really know what I'm working on," he said. "No one really knows." Or as the *Tao Te Ching* says, "Those who know don't talk. Those who talk don't know."

Publicly discussing the flaws in his swing just to appease the press wouldn't much help Tiger in pursuit of his goals. Agreeing with reporters that he is in a slump—when by ordinary standards that is simply not true—is allowing others to define the nature of his challenge. Wallowing in one's mistakes, as some athletes do, makes much less sense than taking what was good and building on it. Yes, Tiger will occasionally admit to playing poorly—"I putted atrociously," he'll say with a smirk, or, "I played like an idiot"—but such negative assessments are rare. Put simply, Tiger believes in the power of positive thinking and positive speech.

Like when a reporter asked him what qualities he did not like in himself—a trick question that can only be answered with a negative thought. Tiger took several long seconds before finding a loophole. "I don't know," he finally said. "I'm constantly evolving."

STILLNESS:
Master Your Senses

"Cultivate Stillness. Breathe harmony. Become tranquility.
As the ten thousand things rise and fall, rise and fall,
Just witness their return to the root."
  —The Tao Te Ching

"A bomb could be going off, you probably wouldn't even know. That's the
focus I had."
  —Tiger Woods

THERE GOES TIGER WOODS, walking to the first tee like he's late for his own wedding. Watch how he cuts a sharp line through the fans gathered to see him, never breaking stride or veering off course. And look, there is his mother, Tida, standing along the path that leads to the first tee at the Augusta National Golf Course, where Tiger is playing in the 2001 Masters. What will Tiger say to her when he sees her? Will there be a hug? A quick kiss? Words of encouragement? A smile or a wink?

There goes Tiger Woods, walking right towards his mother, walking within a few feet of her, walking right up to her, and . . . nothing. Nada. Zilch. Tiger just keeps walking, up to the first tee. It is clear that Tiger did not even see his mother. Never had a clue she was there. The woman who gave birth to Tiger might as well have been a fence post.

Ladies and gentlemen, meet Tiger Woods—or, rather, don't meet him. Your chances of having any kind of meaningful interaction with him on a golf course—or even of making eye contact—are basically zero. When Tiger is playing in a tournament, he is able to exert a surreal control over his senses, deciding for himself what he sees, what he hears, what he feels. Confronted by a blinding wave of distractions and ever-increasing demands on his attention, he is able to maintain a remarkable stillness, slipping into a kind of cocoon even as he is surrounded by thousands of screaming fans. This is the reason TV cameras linger on Tiger long after he has hit a shot and long before he hits the next one—it is utterly mesmerizing to watch him walk a golf course, unaffected by clamor, oblivious to distractions, impervious to all stimuli. "He holds a certain consciousness, the way he goes about things, that is at a higher level than everyone else," says Gary McCord. "There is a kind of aura about him when he's going about his business."

On the golf course, Tiger is simply impenetrable. Most famously he once blew right past his father and Nike CEO Phil Knight—the man who had just signed him to a $40 million endorsement deal—without so much as a flicker of recognition on the way to the first tee at Augusta. At the 2000 British Open, a naked woman streaked across the 18th fairway and green, dancing with the flagstick and catching everyone's eye—everyone, that is, except Tiger, who showed no sign of having noticed her. At the 2000 U.S. Open, Tiger laughed and joked with his caddy on the way to the first tee, until they reached the tee box. Then Tiger lost the smile, put his hand on his driver head cover and stared intently down the fairway for a full two minutes, oblivious to his hollering gallery. He did not emerge from that trancelike state for another five hours.

Beyond his gift for living in the moment and applying megafocus to specific golf shots, Tiger is able to sustain this more general and durable focus that extends the length of a round and, indeed, the length of a tournament. "The week of a major, you have to eat, drink, think, dream—just everything—golf," he once said. "I can get into that totally obsessed state. . . . I know how to focus." In Buddhist thinking, Tiger's centeredness is not so much an obsession as it is a releasing of obsessions—a distillation of the world around him down to its manageable essence. "The ego is a monkey catapulting through the jungle," Lao Tzu tells us. "Totally fascinated by the realm of the senses, it swings from one desire to the next. . . . Let this monkey go. Let the senses go. Let desires go. Let conflicts go. . . . Just remain in the center, watching. And then forget that you are there."

We hold the power to block out distractions and focus on what matters to us, but to do so we must loosen our grips on the things that scare and concern us—we must free our minds from inner distractions before we can eliminate external ones. "Master your senses," says *The Dhammapada*. "What you taste and smell, what you see, what you hear. In all things be a master of what you do and say and think. . . . Are you quiet? Quiet your body. Quiet your mind."

This, Tiger has been able to do with impressive consistency—from the 1994 Pacific Northwest Amateur Championship, when he told his father "I am at peace," and on through his eight majors and dozens of PGA wins. For this reason some people think of Tiger as icy and untouchable, on and off the golf course. He insists it isn't so. "They have this perception of me because of what they see when I play golf," Tiger said in 2004. "I am not that way all the time. I have found a way to maximize my abilities. I have to be this way when I play."

When he plays, he is undoubtedly and deliberately impolite—no "hellos" or "thanks," no small talk with fans, a palpable sheen of superiority, of being above it all. On his face no hint of emotion, no scrunch of passion, no expression at all—just blankness. It is almost as if Tiger wants us to think he is not even there, as if he wishes to be invisible, floating through galleries, silently, stealthily, closed down, inaccessible, entirely remote, existing in some parallel universe. As if Tiger wishes to shrink himself so he can lessen the impact others can have on him. "Subtle and insubstantial, the expert leaves no trace," Sun Tzu says in *The Art of War*. "Divinely mysterious, he is inaudible. Thus, he is master of his enemy's fate."

Of course, all good athletes are capable of blocking out distractions, and all great athletes can do it when they need to most. But Tiger's stillness and sensory command are all the more remarkable considering the sport he plays. In no other sport are fans permitted to cluster so close to the combatants—to stand within three or four feet of the players while they take their shots. What's more, Tiger commands the biggest and densest galleries in almost every event he plays, ensuring that his every swing takes place in a tiny, traveling ampitheater with no seats and only a thin rope to keep hovering fans at bay.

The scrutiny can be crushing, the din of even hushed crowds excruciatingly loud. Sometimes the intrusion is even physical: on the

15th hole at Augusta one year, an overanxious lad approached Tiger just as he had finished a particularly violent swing off a hardpan lie. The recoiling club nearly smashed the young boy on the head, even as the oblivious child reached up to pat Tiger on the shoulder. Tiger's reaction? He stared straight ahead, watching his shot, before following it down the fairway. He apparently never even felt the boy's touch. "Other people are excited, as though they were at a parade," says the *Tao Te Ching*. "I alone don't care. I alone am expressionless, like an infant before it can smile."

Tiger's aloneness brings to mind the steely, robotic focus of golf greats Ben Hogan and Jack Nicklaus. They, too, might as well have been practicing in their backyards when they were playing in tournaments, for all they seemed to notice what was going on around them. And, like Tiger, they had no choice but to be that way because of their relationship with their galleries of fans. Some great athletes feed off adoring crowds, drawing energy from the exhortations of fans and coasting on the torrent of good feelings offered them. Arnold Palmer, whose popularity with fans turned golf into a mainstream sport, is the best example of this.

But Tiger Woods, like Hogan and Nicklaus, does not feed off crowds; he is not empowered by living life in a fishbowl. "He would just as soon do what he does in a hermetically sealed bottle," says Jim Huber. "Muhammad Ali thrived on a crowd, he played to the crowd, but Tiger Woods is the opposite. He never plays to the crowd. The way he entertains is by his commitment and his performance, not by playing to his fans." Indeed, Tiger has never been comfortable in the glare of fame, particularly when the spotlight burned white-hot. Asked in 2004 if he missed all the attention the world paid him during his two best years, Tiger said, "I could care less about the spotlight. I've never been interested in the spotlight. I've been interested in just winning."

That is why Tiger's impenetrability on and around golf courses is so crucial to his success; his immense popularity creates exponentially more challenging conditions in which he has to play. It could even be argued that no athlete in the world has to focus harder and longer than Tiger Woods. Football, basketball and baseball games generally last around three hours. But Tiger must remain focused for five hours a day over four consecutive days, a task made all the more difficult because of the size of his galleries and his aversion to scrutiny and crowds. Blocking out distractions is a central part of Tiger's challenge, and his brilliance derives as much from his ability to do so as from any other virtue. He simply refuses to get swept up in the excitement of the crowd, no matter how forceful its pull.

In mythology, the heroic journey always includes obstacles that can divert a hero from his path; thus heroes have to walk a razor's edge, and any distraction can send them toppling into the abyss. "When you are doing something that is a brand-new adventure, breaking new ground . . . there's always the danger of too much enthusiasm, of neglecting certain mechanical details," Joseph Campbell explained in *The Power of Myth*. "Keep your mind in control, and don't let it pull you compulsively into disaster."

Tiger's stoic serenity and clarity of purpose are traits he now recognizes in young players at his golf clinics. Asked if he sees greatness in some of his charges, Tiger replied, "You don't necessarily see it, but you can feel it. You can definitely feel it. There's a sense—maybe there's an aura they're giving off, or whatever it is, but there's a sense that that kid has something." Stillness, mastery of senses, harmony, inner calm—when you achieve them you create a palpable force field around yourself, buffering you against the harsh elements that would bring you down. "As in the ocean's midmost depth no wave is born, but all is still, so let the practitioner be still," says the *Sutta-Nipata*. "Be motionless, and nowhere should they swell."

Like any virtue, stillness is a discipline that must be practiced and refined. But in Tiger's case, some of his sense mastery is inherent. Even as a baby, he could become exceptionally absorbed by tasks. When he was just a few months old, Tiger would stare spellbound at his father as Earl hit ball after ball into a net in his garage. How long could the infant stay transfixed? Five minutes? Ten minutes? Half an hour? "In the garage, he had an attention span of two hours," says Earl. "He'd watch me hit balls into a net and he wouldn't take his eyes off me." Considering how infants can get distracted by their own spittle, Tiger's early attentiveness seems superhuman.

Then came his father's military training and his mother's Buddhist teachings. Tida was the calming influence, exposing her son to meditation and to Zen masters. "When she was around the golf course, she was there to sort of help calm things down," remembers Wally Goodwin, Tiger's Stanford coach. "If something came up, she always had a great smile on her face, and this had a calming impact on Tiger."

John Andrisani, a frequent writer on Tiger's golf game, has said that Tiger became especially proficient in a form of mediation called *Shamatha*, which can lead to sustained and intense concentration on tasks. Philip Kapleau, in *The Three Pillars of Zen*, sheds light on another form of meditation—Shikan-taza—that can help its practicioners block out distractions. Shikan-taza is "a heightened state of concentrated awareness wherein one is neither tense nor hurried, and certainly never slack," he explains. In discussing the challenges faced by a swordsman in a death duel, Kapleau writes, "Were you to relax your vigilance even momentarily, you would be cut down instantly. A crowd gathers to see the fight. Since you are not blind you see them from the corner of your eye, and since you are not deaf you hear them. But not for an instant is your mind captured by these sense impressions."

There's no question that being steeped in Buddhism helped Tiger master his senses and achieve stillness in a way few athletes ever have. Asked about his mother's influence on his serene demeanor, Tiger said, "Buddhism plays a major role. It has given me the inner peace and calmness I probably would not have achieved at such an early age. I owe that to my mother." But Tiger's father, a former Green Beret, also contributed, administering a heavy dose of military-style training. Among the many psychological tactics employed by Earl: dropping his golf bag, crowing loudly and otherwise causing commotions during Tiger's back swing. Thanks to this training Tiger learned to block out distractions, or at least to not let them interfere with his play. "He just concentrates better than anyone else, and that's why he wins," says Steven Bowen, head pro at Royal Oaks Country Club, site of Tiger's "at peace" triumph in the 1994 Pacific Northwest Amateur Championship. On that day Tiger "was very serious, very quiet. He just handled himself so well. You just have to like his intensity."

Sometimes it seems that Tiger's focus is so intense, his demeanor so flat and devoid of passion, that he has essentially turned himself into a zombie. And where's the fun in that? Indeed, his parents worried early on that Tiger was simply too serious to be enjoying himself while playing. "That's how I enjoy myself, by shooting low scores," young Tiger assured his father. But, in fact, Tiger *was* too intense, and one of the secrets to his sense mastery is that he is *not* fully focused for every second of those five hours on the golf course. Early on, he discovered that maintaining focus depends on abstaining from it from time to time. "My biggest thing as a kid was to learn how to relax on the golf course," he once explained. "Because I used to get too into it. And I used to get tired by the time I got to 13, 14, because I was so focused on what I was doing. And I've learned how to be more relaxed on a golf course in breaking it up. You can't be focused for five straight hours."

Instead, Tiger slips out of his cocoon at carefully planned intervals before slipping back in when he needs to. "It's not like he's in a total shell for five hours," says Roger Maltbie. "Tiger will converse with his fellow competitors and with his caddy. And I think those bursts of concentration are more effective than trying to keep yourself wrapped in a cocoon all day."

Tiger has learned how to set and pre-set his focus during a round, a trick many top athletes possess. Tennis great Bjorn Borg relied on a trigger—spinning his racket—to reset his focus. By trying to maintain focus for five hours, "you can give yourself a headache or burn out or lose your concentration towards the end of the round," Tiger told a 16-year-old golfer who asked if it's unsociable to ignore your playing partner. "Talking to the other players is my way of not overextending my mind by focusing on one thing too long."

Far from shutting down completely, Tiger frequently talks and laughs and gets loose during rounds—and if he doesn't, his caddy Steve makes sure he does. "I followed him during a round at Augusta one year and I remember he missed a fairway with one tee shot and wound up in some pine straw," says Sid Matthew. "So here comes Tiger all serious, and he picks up the pine straw and asks Steve, 'What's this stuff?' And Steve reaches down and grabs a handful and throws it all over Tiger. And Tiger broke out in the biggest smile and the two of them got a big laugh out of that. Of course Tiger then had to brush every bit of pine straw off himself, because he as to look perfect out there."

At Stanford University, Tiger was already adept at dropping in and out of focus—at slipping into his cocoon when he needed to. "All the guys would be in the van from the hotel to the golf course and, boy, did they have fun in there," says their coach, Wally Goodwin. "Always kidding each other, playing practical jokes, riding each other mercilessly. But the second the van door opened at the golf course, dead silence. *Dead silence.* Tiger and his teammates would go right to the putting green and get right to business. They could turn it on and off with great ease."

What Tiger is doing in these instances, says performance expert Dr. Jim Loehr, is selectively disengaging. "We do not have an infinite supply of energy," says Loehr. "Even a fighter pilot on the Blue Angels Precision Flying Team can't maintain concentration without the slightest drop, so he picks his moment when he thinks he can take a breath. He allows this oscillation to happen and then he gets back on track one hundred percent. In golf, there is a time between shots when you can allow concentration and focus to settle into another channel."

The danger, of course, is not being able to reset yourself—succumbing to the distractions. "If you don't have rituals or routines to guide you, you can lose focus altogether and start gabbing with the crowds and all that," says Loehr. "Or you can think too much about something and then you get lost. But Tiger knows just how to invest his energy. He is able to manage the energy impulse."

Tiger's intermittent moments of decreased focus are, of course, tightly controlled. Yes, he likes a laugh now and then with Steve or his playing partner, but Tiger rarely if ever acknowledges anybody else during a round. Reporters and business associates who are allowed to follow Tiger inside the ropes have said that he never so much as glanced at them during 18 holes. "Occasionally, he'll make eye contact with [his wife] Elin in the gallery," says Jim Huber, "but for the most part he looks straight down the fairway. He doesn't interact with anybody except Steve."

Yet despite Tiger's phenomenal tunnel vision, there is one sound in the world that can yank him out of his induced reverie and into the real world. Not the screaming of fans or claps of thunder of even huge airplanes roaring overhead: no, Tiger's kryptonite is the faint whirling click of a camera shutter. Many times Tiger has stopped his swing an instant before impact because of overeager photographers. "He can get rattled," says his former coach John Anselmo. "He'll hear the noise in his back swing and he'll turn around and give the person this bad stare. And, boy, what a look that is. But then he just goes back to doing his thing."

Thus does Tiger do his thing, immersed completely in his task and in total control of his mind and senses. "One who conquers himself," says *The Dhammapada*, "is greater than another who conquers a thousand times a thousand men on the battlefield." We may never be able to attain the stillness of being that Tiger does, but certainly we can use it as inspiration as we try to move closer towards the center of our own lives. After all, one can exert control over one's senses by doing something as simple as shutting off the TV. When we do the things that matter most to us, we must do them fully—we must block out all distractions. Isn't that the lovely lesson behind Tiger's stillness?

Consider Tiger's dream of an ideal round of golf. No galleries, no scoreboards, no clicking shutters—just him, his clubs and balls, and miles of green, green grass. "What I like to do is go out in the evenings and play six, nine holes by myself," Tiger has said. "That's when golf is the coolest."

The beauty of Tiger Woods, of course, is that no matter when he plays, he always plays alone.

FEARLESSNESS:
Take Risks

"You are at your best when your life is fraught with danger. You find your strength in reacting to the dangers that beset you. Since you are most effective when under pressure, the dangerous elements of a situation enhance it for you."
—*I Ching interpretation*

"I refuse to give in to fear. . . . In order to be truly successful in any endeavor, you have to adopt a no-fear attitude. Don't be afraid to go for it."
—*Tiger Woods*

ONE OF THE COMBATANTS WAS SAM SNEAD, the retired PGA superstar with a record 81 wins in his career. The other: some six-year-old squirt named Tiger Woods. The setting was an exhibition match at Soboba Springs Royal Vista Golf Course in San Jacinto, California—a friendly little game between a legend and a prodigy. On the very first hole, a 200-yard par 3, young Tiger struck a lovely shot with his driver but—being only six—failed to reach the green. Instead his ball slid down a steep bank and towards a greenside pond. It settled on the edge of the water, halfway submerged.

The next move was a no-brainer: take the ball out of the water and play from a dry lie. After all, this was an exhibition match with nothing on the line—no reason for this little kid to try such a difficult shot. Why then, wondered the great Snead, was Tiger lurking around the pond, scoping out the shot? "Sam goes up to him and says, 'Tiger, go ahead, just take it out of the water,'" remembers Rudy Duran, who was Tiger's swing coach at the time and a member of that day's foursome. "But I can tell that Tiger is thinking, 'This is a playable shot.' So he just shrugged off what Sam suggested and went about his business and set up over the shot and looked up at the green and smacked the ball out of the water. And the ball landed right in the middle of the green."

The impertinence of youth? Some might call it that. But in light of everything Tiger has accomplished—he is on track to eclipse Snead's 81 wins—it's more likely Tiger was already flashing one of his calling cards: fearlessness. Throughout his career, Tiger has shown a willingness—even an eagerness—to take extraordinary risks. He has relished the opportunity to attempt perilous shots that would make most golfers tremble. He has routinely gone for broke with a gambler's abandon, undaunted by bad lies, steel-wool rough, treacherous footing or inconvenient trees. He would rather chug castor oil than accept a penalty stroke. "I don't think I have ever seen anybody take the chances he takes to make a shot happen," says his former swing coach John Anselmo. "And these are risky shots I'm talking about. My God, are they risky shots."

In any round of golf, there will be situations that force a player to contemplate risk versus reward. Is the payoff of pulling out a miracle shot worth the risk of disaster should something go wrong? Sure, a ball nestled in pine cones behind a tree 200 yards from the green can, conceivably, be smashed, knocked-down or hooked so that, somehow, it finds its way towards the flag. But it can also ricochet off the tree and wind up deeper in the woods. Is saving one stroke worth risking two or three or maybe more? Is it worth introducing the possibility of a round-ruining triple bogey? Most amateur golfers—with nothing to lose except maybe a five-dollar bet—will go the safe route and avoid playing risky shots, choosing instead to chip back into the fairway or declare the lie unplayable. They understand their skill levels and do not feel comfortable pushing the envelope.

Professional golfers, on the other hand, confront the same risk/reward situations with hundreds of thousands of dollars on the line. And yet, you will often see pros attempt impossibly risky shots, convinced their talents will shift unfriendly odds in their favor.

But even among this courageous elite, one golfer stands out—Tiger Woods. Regardless of the situation, Tiger's instinct is to disregard risk and play every shot full out, and he has succeeded far more often than he has failed. "Tiger is truly a fearless shot maker," says Bobby

Clampett. "He knows his abilities and he knows what he can do, and he loves the challenge of trying to pull off the great shot. And he knows that he can pull it off more often than anyone else can."

In the final round of the 2001 Memorial, Tiger was paired with Paul Azinger, who was leading him by one as they came to the par-5 fourth hole. For his second shot Azinger had 247 yards to the pin, which sat only 10 feet from the front of the green. Miss short and he'd be in the pond that fronted the green. The safe play was to lay up or at least hit it way right of the pin, where there was no water. Aiming at the flag was extremely risky. Still, Azinger took out a 3-wood and went pin-hunting. He put a good swing on his ball but pulled it slightly left; it came up short and sank into the pond.

Tiger hit next. He was 240 yards from the flag and hit a towering 3-iron, which ignored the abyss and settled six feet from the cup. Azinger chipped up and two-putted for bogey; Tiger canned his eagle putt. He went from one behind to leading by two and never looked back, eventually winning by seven strokes. "Every day Tiger plays, he hits one or two shots that nobody else would even attempt, let alone execute," CBS golf analyst Peter Oosterhaus marveled at the time.

Knowing this, did Azinger feel pressure to attempt a risky shot he might otherwise have not played? Did Tiger's fearlessness factor into his decision? "Why Tiger won so often early in his career was that he forced other players—fabulous players—to try the same shots he hit," says David Feherty. "He made them bite off more than they could chew. Most of those shots were just too big a gamble for these other players. But not for Tiger. He is capable of doing things no one else on this planet can do." Some players have even admitted that Tiger's daring forces them out of their own games. "I've gotten at times to feel like I've had to do something almost supernatural when I'm playing against him," Davis Love III, one of the top ten players of his generation, once remarked. "I'm trying too hard, trying to be something you're not instead of just playing."

Tiger, put simply, is comfortable taking risks. He has even introduced risk where none existed. In the final round of the 2001 AT&T National Pro-Am at Pebble Beach, he trailed the leader, Matt Gogel, by four strokes with four to play. To give himself a chance to win, he would have to play aggressively, but not recklessly. Then came his second shot on the par four 15th hole. He only had 97 yards, but the pin was on a small shelf in the back right of the green. His normal 97-

yard shot, a lob wedge, would likely spin back too much to stay up on the shelf. But any other club would surely travel too far to stay on the green. Tiger needed to do something special to give himself a reasonable shot at birdie.

And he had just the thing: the dead-arms shot. It was something he had been working on with his then-coach, Butch Harmon—a tricky, nuanced shot where he took a softer, quieter swing to eliminate spin. Executed just right, the shot would drop out of the sky and land on a dime. Hit a little wrong, it would sail 20 or 30 yards over the green. The problem was that Tiger had never tried the shot in competition. Hauling it out at such a crucial moment in the final round was, to say the least, fraught with risk. Then again, Tiger is "more willing to bring a shot from the practice tee onto the course than any golfer I know," Harmon has said of his former pupil.

Standing alongside the fairway during that final round and watching Tiger contemplate that difficult second shot, Harmon wondered if Tiger would have the nerve to try his new swing. Sure enough, Tiger dead-armed the shot, which landed gingerly three feet from the hole and spun ever so slightly, trickling down the shelf. It didn't stop near the cup, it stopped dab-smack *in* the cup for eagle. "I was with Matt Gogel a couple of holes behind Tiger when that second shot went in," remembers David Feherty. "We heard this absolute roar come up and we both knew right away it was for Tiger. We also knew that it was not good news for Matt." Following his miracle eagle, a pumped-up Tiger made two more birdies and wound up winning by two. "After that incredible shot," says Feherty, "Tiger was like a tsunami coming in at 600 miles an hour."

Tiger's bold decisions in these make-or-break moments paid off handsomely for him, just as taking risks in key situations can pay off for anyone. In fact, stepping beyond our comfort levels and welcoming occasional forays into the unknown are essential to feeling fully alive. "It's important to live life with the experience, and therefore the knowledge, of its mystery and of your own mystery," Joseph Campbell explained in *The Power of Myth*. "This gives life a new radiance, a new harmony, a new splendor." By taking risks, "you learn to recognize the positive values in what appear to be the negative moments and aspects of your life. The big question is whether you are going to be able to say a hearty 'Yes!' to your adventure."

Say yes to your adventure—what lovely advice. To do otherwise is to deprive yourself of the fullness and richness of being alive. Indeed, the Buddhist concept of Nirvana does not refer to an abstract place such as heaven, but rather to a state of mind attained when we are released from desire and fear. To be afraid—to say "no" to your adventure—is to be stuck in a sad and unharmonious life, something no one wants. "I have never encountered an individual who would be satisfied with a tombstone that said, 'He Was Ordinary,'" says performance expert Jim Loehr. "What everybody wants is to be extraordinary in the things that matter to them. Inside all of us is this yearning to make a difference."

Tiger understands that true greatness can only be achieved by taking risks. Of course, he also knows that not every risk he takes will pay off. Quite a few along the way will produce dispiriting results. Being able to shrug off those setbacks is what allows Tiger to be so bold in the first place—he is able to embrace risk because he is not afraid of failure. And the reason he is not afraid to fail is because he has no interest in being perfect. Watching Tiger on the golf course, we might make the mistake of thinking he is chasing perfection. After all, everything he does during a round, every movement, every decision, is geared towards producing the best result possible. But that is not the same as aspiring to perfection; Tiger knows there is no such thing. To enter a round of golf with the goal of making no mistakes is to cripple yourself with the fear of doing just that. Trying to be perfect inhibits risk-taking and makes true greatness impossible to reach. "I really don't believe that there is such a thing as perfection because we are human," Tiger said in 1999. "I have always been a big believer in professional excellence, and that is what I try and achieve. I know I can never get to a point where I hit perfect shots every time."

In other words, the point is not to successfully execute every risky shot you take—no one can do that. The point is to embrace risk and have the guts to attempt such shots in the first place. "Sometimes I pull it off and other times I don't," Tiger once said, "but if you want to win, you gotta go." Sure, you will make your share of mistakes, but every mistake is a chance to learn something and gather crucial information for the next go-around. "Failure is an opportunity," the *Tao Te Ching* tells us. "The master fulfills his own obligations and corrects his own mistakes." With Tiger, "he really got to the point where he took a bad shot as a challenge," says his

Stanford coach Wally Goodwin. "He would say, 'Coach, I hit it in the trees and I love going over there because I can get it out.' And hitting it as long as he did, his ball went into some really strange places. Some of the shots he hit were probably never hit before."

Bob Rottella, the gifted golf psychologist, notes that while a majority of golfers say they love the sport for its challenges, most will frown and fret when faced with bad lies. Isn't that the very thing that drew them to golf—the challenge of making a great shot in a bad situation? Shouldn't risky plays be approached with guts and gusto? Of course, human nature tends to take over on a golf course, and it is only natural to view deep bunker shots or four-irons over water with trepidation. We can't tell our hearts to stop beating fast. We can, however, learn to adjust our approach to such shots and, in essence, impose our will on the situation.

Like many things in golf, and in life, it is a mental trick. "Tiger's father told him that in every round you will hit one shot that will never be forgotten in the history of golf—one truly great shot," says Jim Loehr. "So that when Tiger gets himself in a bad situation with an impossible lie, I am sure what is going through his head is, 'This is my shot.' It is very hard to hit a truly great shot from the middle of the fairway. But the one that is buried in the deep grass, that you have to curve it low under a tree—that is the shot that brings out the greatness in Tiger. And he thinks, 'This is where I separate myself from everyone else.'"

That sort of thinking requires a willingness to step outside our comfort zones. We all feel much better facing a shot we know we can hit—a shot we have executed successfully many times before. But the beauty of golf is that it will likely force us out of our comfort zone several times a round. When we can embrace these moments, rather than dread them, we will have found a new pathway to the extraordinary.

Tiger understood this at an early age, thanks to the teachings of his father Earl. When Tiger was young and playing primarily at the Heartwell Golf Park in Long Beach, California, Earl took the scorecard and assigned new pars for his son. Some were par 6s, some 7s, depending on their length. "Earl already knew what Tiger could shoot, and he made it so Tiger would always be able to shoot under par," says his high school coach Don Crosby. This at first seems counterintuitive—why not make it so that Tiger had to work harder to break par? Earl's goal, however, was to acclimate Tiger to shooting low scores. "As a result Tiger has basically spent his whole life shooting under par," says Crosby.

This method also allowed Earl to occasionally force Tiger out of his comfort zone. "All of a sudden I would change one of the pars from a 7 to a 6," says Earl. "And when I changed the pars those were some of the biggest arguments Tiger and I ever had in our life. But then he would go out there and still shoot under par." Says Don Crosby, "Most of us have never been consistently under par, so when we get there we want to stay there and we play defensively. But Earl had Tiger under par his whole life, so he learned he always had to go even lower and be aggressive."

Earl's trick basically obliterated the concept of any comfort zone for Tiger at all. What mattered was getting the birdie, going low—beating the golf course. This allowed him to approach risk in an entirely positive way—to view dangerous situations as a chance to discover his true character. "It is a warrior's mentality," says Gary McCord. "Tiger is never going to give up on a shot."

In this way, perhaps, Tiger recalls the Samurai warriors of 14th and 15th century China. They learned not only to be unafraid of death but to embrace the concept and keep it in mind at all times, so that they were able to be truly appreciative of life. Stripped of any fear, they became fierce fighters and ruled China for several centuries. Learning to become unafraid of failure clears the way to taking risks and improves our chances of succeeding. "If a warrior is not unattached to life and death, he will be of no use whatsoever," says *Hagakure: The Book of the Samurai.* "With such non-attachment one can accomplish any feat."

HAPPY WARRIOR:
Do Not Fear Success

"To accept destiny is to face life with open eyes. Whereas not to accept destiny is to face death blindfolded."
— The Tao Te Ching

"I've heard of players being afraid to win. Imagine that."
— Tiger Woods

YOU WANT PRESSURE? You want knee-knocking, mouth-drying nervousness? Try standing on the first tee of your very first professional tournament, with hundreds of fans crowded around you on the tee box and hundreds more lining each side of the 447-yard first fairway, all to watch you kick off the most hyped and anticipated career in decades—*and* you're all of 20 years old. That was the spooky situation Tiger Woods faced at the 1996 Greater Milwaukee Open, at 8:28 in the morning of his first day as a pro. How could he not be shaking in his spikes?

In fact, there *was* a moment when Tiger felt the crushing weight of expectations, but it was decidedly not on the first tee that day. "He just seemed so comfortable with it, like he was used to it," remembers Tom Strong, the tournament director at the GMO that year. "I'm sure he was nervous but he handled it very professionally." Tiger would later recall that he was aware of, but not overwhelmed by, the pressure of that inaugural shot. "I swear it felt like it took about fifteen seconds for that club to get to the top of my swing," he said. "It was so heavy. I have never experienced anything like that in my life. But I got through it." Indeed: Tiger smashed his drive 336 yards, birdied his first hole as a pro and birdied two of the next four as well. So much for nerves.

No, the moment when Tiger felt punched in the gut by the prospect of his destiny came a day before the first round, at the tournament's press conference. "He realized he was in uncharted waters, and he had to face all these reporters, and not all of them were friendly, and he had to learn a lot of things about being a pro," says his father, Earl, who sat behind Tiger's podium at the press conference. "He knew his life would never be the same after that moment. And if you watch the video of the press conference, you can see that Tiger suddenly reaches back to me and extends his hand. And I reached forward and took his hand, and we held hands as he went on with the interviews."

Tiger was right to think his life would be forever changed. He was only doing what any 20-year-old might do when he sought a little comfort from his dad that day. Yet after Tiger's touching, utterly human display of apprehension, he would never again betray the slightest hint that he was not ready for his task. From there on in, Tiger never showed even a trace of ambivalence about his chosen goal. Essentially from the moment Tiger embarked on his journey towards greatness, he never once shrank from the obligations and rigors of being what he was determined to be: the most dominant and influential athlete of his time. Quite the contrary, Tiger embraced his top-dog status and everything—good and bad—that it entailed. "Tiger absolutely craves success," says Jim Huber. "He very much believes in himself and in what he is doing. He is very, very comfortable with success."

In this, Tiger brilliantly illustrates an often-overlooked virtue: he has no fear of success. In sports, as in life, an athlete's fear of succeeding can be far more crippling than his or her fear of coming up short. Players can become concerned with the trappings of success—how their lives might change, how the extra attention might affect their performance, how success might turn out to be more of a burden than a boon. As a result, they might subconsciously sabotage themselves in their pursuit of greatness, ensuring that the relatively comfortable existence they currently enjoy will not undergo a radical change. They resist examining the true depths of their talents, and shirk—sometimes imperceptibly—away from the full measure of their skills. Being enamored of our potential, after all, is far less frightening than actually achieving it.

For this reason, some exceptional athletes find different ways to lose when victory lies well within reach. "Because of the enormous stress associated with success, their performance suffers; they become erratic and inconsistent," write Chungliang Al Huang and Jerry Lynch in *Thinking Body, Dancing Mind*, citing Sigmund Freud's essay, "Those Wrecked by Success." Even for some athletes who have experienced being the best, "success becomes an albatross . . . so weighty and strangling that they avoid it at all costs."

In Tiger's case, the heaviness of success is even greater: he must shoulder all the expectations that come with being the first black golfer to have reached the pinnacle of his sport. Tiger was a role model before he was a legal adult, stripped of his anonymity and privacy before he really had an understanding of what that meant. "Tiger has a responsibility on his shoulders more than any other golfer by a million miles," eight-time major winner Gary Player has observed.

Which makes everything that Tiger has accomplished all the more remarkable: he has faced larger-than-life challenges and risen to the occasion every time. Indeed, Tiger simply has no interest in settling for anything less than his true and full potential, regardless of the consequences for his personal life. "Tiger is not afraid of anything," says his father Earl "Some people say things like, 'I can't see myself as the president of this corporation.' And so they have no chance to be president. They are afraid to succeed. But Tiger is not afraid of failure and he's not afraid of success."

For some, the fear of success comes from facing the unknown. Mediocrity is a good armchair, its comfort familiar and dependable. But success is a mysterious entity, at once enticing and utterly terrifying. Tiger's advantage is that, because of his Buddhist upbringing, he has an understanding of the impermanence of success. Everywhere in Buddhist literature we are reminded that those who taste success are bound to then experience failure—in other words, what goes up must come down. "Amass possessions, establish positions, display your pride," says the *Tao Te Ching*. "Soon enough disaster drives you to your knees." This is just the way of the world, a natural leveling of tides. Fortunes that rise must inevitably fall. Tiger knows his fortunes will rise and fall several times throughout his career. His periods of diminished efficiency may frustrate him, but they never surprise him. Prosperity's built-in trap door doesn't faze Tiger; he is enamored of the *experience* of chasing his potential, in all its gore and glory. "A lot of times when a guy is in the hunt, he does not look comfortable or like he's enjoying himself," says Roger Maltbie. "But you watch Tiger and you can always tell that he is right where he wants to be. He's saying, 'This is what I train for, this is why I do what I do. Maybe this isn't fun for you, but it sure is fun for me.'"

It is one thing to be the best player in your sport. It is another to be the best player in your sport by a whole bunch. But even during the years when Tiger was statistically leaps and bounds ahead of his closest rivals—when he was not just the top dog but, it seemed, the *only* dog—he never recoiled from his supremacy. "Our deepest fear is not that we are inadequate. Our deepest fear is that we are powerful beyond measure," Nelson Mandela once said. "It is our light, not our darkness, that most frightens us."

To give in to this fear, however, is to deny the heroic impulse that resides in us all. There is nothing noble about underachieving or, as Mandela put it, "playing small." Only the bold and determined pursuit of our potential can be considered good and right. Our individual battles to achieve greatness are actually part of society's bigger battle to discover the greatness in itself. When we bravely face our destinies, we create a shining example that serves to pull others along for the ride. And so when you venture to unleash your own potential "you save the world," observed Joseph Campbell in *The Power of Myth*. "The influence of a vital person vitalizes, there's no doubt about it." This perfectly summarizes the appeal of Tiger Woods: he is a vitalized person whose influence has and continues to vitalize the many people who cross his path.

In sports, all professional athletes have to some degree pursued their greatness. Had they felt a gnawing fear of success, they surely would have folded long before becoming part of their sport's elite. Even the 12th guy on a pro basketball team is living out the wildest dreams of a million men and boys. Even the third-string cornerback is rich, revered and a role model back home.

But within this culture there is still a gulf between the very good players and the truly great ones. Becoming the top performer in your sport does not happen by accident; to be the very best you must desire it desperately. Needless to say, you must have no fear of success. "I did a commentary once about how Phil Mickelson reminded me of Mats Wilander," says Jim Huber. "When Mats was one of the great tennis players in the world and challenging John McEnroe, he flat out said, 'I don't want to be number one. I don't want the hassles or the pressure, and I will be very satisfied being number two in the world.'" In a 2002 interview Phil Mickelson was asked if, like Tiger, his goal was to be the greatest player who ever lived. "Not like that," he admitted. "Not with the kind of focus [Tiger] put into it. To me, there are more important things in life than winning a bunch of majors. . . . I don't want to shortchange myself or my potential. But it's not like I've been one-dimensional in my approach to the game, that the one and only thing is to become the greatest player of all time."

Two years later, Mickelson rededicated himself, revamped his game, improved his conditioning and finally won his first major, the 2004 Masters.

No one can accuse Phil Mickelson of fearing success. He has won at every level, banked millions in prize money and played well enough to be consistently ranked among the top handful of golfers in the world. By any standard he is dazzlingly successful. But is it possible that, for valid reasons, he did not zealously pursue his true and full potential? That he may have indeed shortchanged himself?

These are questions that will never be asked of Tiger Woods. From the beginning he was trained to think of himself as a champion, by parents who were convinced he was destined for greatness. When Tida tried to dispose of the old high chair that Tiger clambered down from to take his first swing in the garage, Earl stopped her. "That's going to be in the Hall of Fame someday," he proclaimed. When young Tiger arrived at Western High School he was the No. 1 junior player in California, and so it was inevitable that he would supplant the much-older leaders on the Western team. "I had this one kid who worked really hard and was sure he was going to be the No. 1 guy on the team as a senior," says Western's golf coach Don Crosby. "But then he saw Tiger play. And he said, 'Coach, I'll never be number one, will I?' And I said, 'Nope, but you'll be a helluva number two.'"

As for Tiger, "he had no fear of being the top guy, even though he was much younger than the other kids," says Crosby. "He had been beating older kids for a long time, so he was used to always being the top dog." The same scenario played out when Tiger enrolled at Stanford University. "He was comfortable being the best player, and he just went along playing his game," says his college coach, Wally Goodwin. "I'm sure there were some kids that didn't want that pressure, but the kids who stood out were not afraid to succeed. They understood that in life there is only one really negative experience and that's dying. Every other experience is not negative as long as you learn something from it."

When Tiger turned pro he wore a bright red shirt during every final round, at the urging of his mother, Tida, who believed red was her son's power color. Some might have seen the shirt as showy or arrogant, but Tiger was not deterred by the extra attention it drew. He not only lived up to the demands of proclaiming himself a Sunday warrior, he far surpassed them.

Some of that confidence undoubtedly stems from the fact that Tiger's mission extends beyond the game of golf. He has always said his true passion is helping children through his Foundation, which means he is playing as much for others as he is for himself. "In every instance where we have an athlete who is connected deeply to their values, we see that that connection is extremely important," says Dr. Jim Loehr. "They are driven not just by surface or expedient choices but are instead deeply connected to powerful forces that guide them in their actions. These forces are way beyond self-interest. There's no question that Tiger sees his life as having much more dimension and value beyond what he does on the golf course. But he also knows that if he doesn't get it done on the golf course, he can't make the statement anywhere else."

If it is human nature to fear success, it is a sign of an enlightened mind not to be chased away from challenges. For inspiration in our quest for greatness, we need look no further than Tiger Woods. At every turn he has stared down the hissing dragons of fear and uncertainty, then slayed them with his mighty Ping or Titleist. "I remember one time we had a long driving competition with some other schools," says Don Crosby. "And we had this one kid on our team, a Hawaiian kid, he was a bomber; my goodness, he could really hit it. So he had the longest drive at one pint, and then it was Tiger's turn."

With the sun quickly setting on the driving range at the Rancho Canada golf course, young Tiger might have let his teammate take the long drive title. He might have walloped his drive without *really* walloping his drive. He might not have summoned every ounce of strength in his skinny body just to win a silly competition. He was already the best golfer on the team—indeed, the entire state. Did he really have to be the longest hitter, too? "Well, Tiger hits and he just comes out of his shoes, he hit it so hard," says Crosby. "It was getting dark and we couldn't see the ball, so we had a guy at the other end of the range with a walkie-talkie. And we hear the guy say, 'Well, that one went over my head and into the water, so I'm not sure how far it was.' And the Hawaiian kid goes, 'Aw, Tiger, for God's sake, you wouldn't even let me win this?'"

"Tiger has always thrived on challenges," says Crosby. "He has just always wanted to be the best."

INTUITION:
Trust Your Gift

"The world is won by letting things
Take their own course."
    —*The Tao Te Ching*

"Just be yourself."
    —*Tiger Woods*

"WHAT ARE YOU THINKING ABOUT when you swing?" young Tiger was once asked by his father. The pin? The green? The yardage? The lie? Tiger's response was simple: "Where I want the ball to go."

Even at an early age Tiger showed a keen understanding of a basic principal of successful performance: true greatness comes only when we stop thinking and trust our gifts. To perform at high levels, an athlete must consistently rely on intuition—the direct perception of truths and facts, independent of the reasoning process. Before his swing, Tiger's analysis of the factors and conditions that will affect his shot is intense and thorough. But during the swing his mind is not consumed by yardage calculations, wind directions or even specific visual targets. Rather, judging by his comments over the years, he streamlines his thoughts into a single mental image that is not so much a target as a simple command: hit the ball where you want it to go.

This is because, at the moment of impact, all the thinking in the world will not get the job done. "Some people think they are concentrating," the great Bobby Jones once said, "when they're merely worrying." Success depends on trusting one's abilities, on letting things take their course. "Evolved individuals know without going about," says the *Tao Te Ching*, "recognize without looking, achieve without acting." Tiger's ability to liberate his mind and perform intuitively is highly evolved. "Tiger is extremely technical about his swing until he sets foot on the golf course," says David Feherty. "And then, like all great players, he's not *trying* to do anything, he's *allowing* himself to do what he has taught his body to do."

Intuitive action is one of the cornerstones of Zen and Buddhist thinking, and having a Buddha Mind—or Beginner's Mind—means trusting the mind to act on its own. "Can you give the wisdom of your heart precedence over the learning of your head?" wonders Lao Tzu. As scholar Alan Watts explains in *The Way of Zen*, "There must be a lag or distance between the source of information and the source of action. When a human being is so self-conscious, so self-controlled that he cannot let go of himself, he dithers and wobbles between opposites."

In sports, as in life, trying too hard to make something happen—steering a golf shot, for instance—rarely leads to success. Phil Jackson, the great basketball coach who won nine championships with the Chicago Bulls and the Los Angeles Lakers, encouraged his players to adopt a Zen-like approach to the game. Jackson's success derived in part from his faith in the innovative Triangle Offense, a free-wheeling, intuitive playing style developed by basketball guru Tex Winter. "[A good shooter] plays and shoots with aplomb," Winter wrote of his offense, "which frees his mind and body to perform the task at hand with relaxed abandon."

Due to his Bhuddhist upbringing, Tiger has a knack for acting with abandon. "I don't think about things that much," he said in 2000. "I watch, I absorb and then I follow instinct." Despite his unmatched work ethic, passionate intensity and technical precision, there is a languor and simplicity to Tiger's play—he makes golf look easy. "It's like trying to catch a butterfly," says David Feherty. "If you snatch at it, you're going to kill it. So what you do is you hold out your palm and let it land there. And that's what Tiger does on the golf course. I have never seen him look like he's trying hard out there." So refined is his reliance on intuition that his former coach Butch Harmon once said, "Even if you put a blindfold on Tiger he could still win."

Harmon may not have been kidding. Consider Tiger's remarkable blind shot on the final hole of the 2001 NEC Invitational—one of the most exhilarating shots in the history of golf. With darkness descending over the Firestone Golf Club in Akron, Ohio, the last few golfers on the course were given the option to suspend play and continue the following morning. Tiger, leading comfortably with only a couple of holes to go, declined the offer. By the time he reached the par four 18th hole, Tiger was playing in almost total darkness. Standing over his second shot, 180 yards away from the flag, he could not even make out the green. "It was pitch black," remembers tournament director Tom Strong, who was huddled around the green that night. "We could not see Tiger in the fairway."

Tiger calculated his yardage, considered his lie and finally selected a pitching wedge. Then, unable to see his target, he let instinct take over. "We heard the shot when he hit it, and the next thing we know we heard the ball land on the green," says Strong. "And everybody is looking around trying to find it. And there it was, *a foot and a half from the flag*. Everybody just went nuts." Fans around the green, flashing cigarette lighters rock concert-style, understood they had witnessed something magical. "From the time Tiger hit that shot to the time we finally saw him walk on the green, it was just a roar," says Strong. "Everybody kept clapping and yelling. It just gave me chills."

How was Tiger able to execute such a miraculous shot? Was he just lucky, or was something else at work? "He was able to hit it because he was totally committed to the shot," says his father Earl. "There was no question of, 'I have to hit it a little harder,' or anything like that. He fed all the information in, he knew his alignment was there, he wasn't worried about the direction. All he had to do was put a solid swing on it, and he knew it. He trusted his ability." Over the years, Earl Woods had consistently implored Tiger to "trust it," to the point where Tiger would hear his father's words in his mind in critical spots. After gutting out a spectacular win at the 1999 PGA Championship at the Medinah Golf Club in greater Chicago, Tiger hugged his father at a reception in the clubhouse. The two had not spoken during the round, but still Tiger whispered to his father, "I heard you, Pop."

Tiger's blind shot is a dramatic example of intuition at work, but his reliance on instinct is on display in every round he plays. One of the very best putters in the game, Tiger "putts instinctively," explains his father, who taught his son the technique when Tiger was barely out of diapers. "He didn't know an inch from a mile, so I couldn't say you have a 10-inch stroke or a two-foot putt. Instead, I taught Tiger to putt to a picture. You look at the hole until you get a clear picture of it, and then the mind calculates on its own how hard to hit the putt."

Most golfers are far more analytical in their approach to putting, applying different formulas to determine the speed of the putt and how far to pull back the putter. Tiger's analysis of greens, slopes and contours is very focused and precise, but when it comes time to pull the trigger all his thinking stops. "Reporters would ask him how long this or that birdie putt was, and he would have to say, 'I don't know,'" says Earl. "He didn't think about how hard to hit the putt, all he did was putt to a picture. Tiger bought into the system when he was one year old, so he had nothing to fight against. Still, learning to trust it is a discipline. You have to learn to trust your stroke."

It is not an exact science, to be sure. Tiger's caddy, Steve Williams, can often be heard exhorting his boss to "trust that good swing of yours." But even Tiger allows self-doubt to creep in from time to time. Late in 2003, he seemed to lose his keenly developed sense of intuition and began over thinking shots. The result was a sustained period of poor driving. "When I get over the shot I feel comfortable," he said after one particularly frustrating round full of badly pulled drives. "I feel I know what I'm doing, *and then I don't trust it*. When you get up there on a shot . . . I'm thinking, 'Okay, I feel great on this shot.' Then as soon as I come down, it's 'Oh no, don't hit it right.' Then you flip it left. Something like that has been happening a lot. I feel like I'm in a good position, I just don't trust it."

Hey, if Tiger doesn't always trust *his* swing, what chance do we have? In fact, Tiger's struggles only prove that learning to trust our gifts takes effort and commitment. The first step is believing in the amazing power of the mind, so that we can *stop trying* and *start acting*. When he was young, Tiger had a poster of Obi-Wan Kenobi—keeper of the mystical Force from *Star Wars*—up on his closet door. Thanks to his mother and father, he appreciated his own Force—his

inner gift—from an early age. "It's something I've begun to understand more," he said in 2000. "I'm learning how to harness it and
protect it a little more. And how to make it grow."

When Tiger has "it" going—when he is performing at his most
intuitive—it is a truly marvelous thing to behold. Who can forget his
exhilarating 1999 Nike commercial, in which he juggles a ball on the
face of his club 49 times before swinging at it in mid-air and hitting
a perfect shot? Tiger bounces the ball between his legs, behind his
back, around his body, everywhere—it is a dazzling display of his vir-
tuosity, and of his intuitive acumen. Conceived when producers
noticed Tiger fooling around with a ball during a break on another
commercial, it required only four takes to complete. In the first three
takes, the commercial's director let Tiger know when there were 10
seconds left, so he could prepare to hit the ball in midair. But that
caused Tiger to think too much about what he was doing and flub
the shot. For the fourth take he asked the director not to give him
more than a few seconds notice, freeing his mind to flawlessly execute the trick. Forty-nine bounces, by the way, is hardly Tiger's
record: he once tapped a ball off his driver 1,000 times.

Tiger's instinctual agility was impressive in that 28-second spot,
but over all four rounds of the 2000 U.S. Open at Pebble Beach, it
was downright mystifying. In that tournament, the first of three
majors he won that year, Tiger gave what appeared to be an utterly
effortless performance, improbably coasting to victory on an exacting course by a record 15 strokes. He strolled Pebble's oceanfront
fairways as if on a weekend retreat, untroubled by obstacles, unfazed
by pressure, completely at one with his gift. "It was actually kind of
boring, because he blew everyone away," says TNT's golf essayist Jim
Huber. "But at the same time you could not stop watching, because
that tournament was when we truly realized we are in the presence
of something very extraordinary. We all sort of knew already, but
Tiger's play at the 2000 U.S. Open really solidified it." Afterwards,
Tiger could only shrug his shoulders when asked about his easy victory. "I just had this serene feeling," he explained. "I knew that if I just
went out there and played my game, I was going to be all right."

What matters, Tiger understands, is not the condition of the
course, the difficulty of the greens, the pressure of the event, or any
external factor—what matters is the state of his mind. Tiger's ability
to stop thinking and fully trust his gift allows him to perform with

an unrivaled intuitive ease. It is like the Zen koan in which two monks are arguing about a flag. "The flag is moving," one of them says. "The wind is moving," says the other. Then a wiser man happens by the argument. "Not the wind, not the flag," says the man, "the *mind* is moving."

DILIGENCE:
Strive Always

"The immature lose their vigilance,
But the wise guard it as their greatest treasure.
Do not fall into ways of sloth."
    —*The Dhammapada*

"I can tell you one thing. This is something I've said and will continue to
say. I'm going to try to get better."
    —*Tiger Woods*

DARKNESS TURNED THE DRIVING RANGE into a lunar landscape, desolate save for a single golfer and his faithful caddie. Tucked away at the far end of the range, the golfer pummeled ball after ball into the dimming sky, long after other players had zipped up their bags and ordered filet mignon. Visitors to the Valhalla Golf Club might have been surprised to discover that the lone golfer in the twilight was, at the time, *leading* the 2000 PGA Championship after three rounds of play. "You could still see a little but it was getting really tough," remembers TNT's golf analyst Jim Huber, who set up his lights and cameras at the other end of the driving range to tape a wrap-up show that evening. "And there's Tiger, leading the championship, out hitting balls until he gets it just right."

Halfway through Huber's show, it got too dark to even see Tiger anymore. That's when Huber noticed golf balls sailing over his head towards a nearby chipping green partially illuminated by his camera lights. "Tiger is lobbing wedges over my head, into the light," marvels

Huber. "I mean, everybody else is long gone to dinner, and here's Tiger squeezing out the last bit of light from the day, then using any light source he can to hit more balls. And after that he went to the putting green for another half-hour."

This is the unquantifiable X-factor in Tiger's play—an insatiable appetite for improving his game. As tempting as it is to think of Tiger as a natural talent, blessed with awesome gifts and a freakish physique that allow him to coast to win after win, it is far more accurate to describe him as a grinder—someone who owes his success primarily to an impeccable work ethic. Most remarkable of all is that Tiger's ferocious desire to improve has not diminished. Indeed, it has intensified with each major championship he has collected. This insistence on continuous improvement—what the Japanese call *kaizen*—leads Tiger to push himself to the breaking point over and over, studiously searching for flaws he can isolate and fix. "Tiger is an extraordinary talent with an extraordinary drive," says Bobby Clampett. "You don't see too many people with that combination. Jack Nicklaus had the drive, but he never had the talent Tiger has."

All professional golfers tinker with their swings and devote countless hours to getting better. To stand pat in the world of pro golf is to allow whole herds of hard-charging players to trample right over you. But Tiger's utter devotion to improving his game—a defining characteristic since he first hoist a fairway wood—is all the more amazing given that, for his whole life, Tiger has not only been the best golfer at his level, but the best golfer *by far*. Such sustained dominance, one might think, could lead a golfer to believe he had earned a break from the rigors of constant practice. Yet despite overwhelming the competition at every step, Tiger has not allowed his work habits to slacken. Tiger's very notion of being successful is based not on wins and losses but on his ability to improve each and every year he plays. "My goal was to be a better player on December 31 than I was on January 1 of the same year," he said in 2003. "If I can keep doing that every year, I think I'm going to have a pretty good record."

Motivated not by prizes and purses but by the pursuit of his own potential, Tiger treats the practice range like a hallowed testing ground, daring himself to dig ever deeper, to work ever harder. Like Igjugarjuk, the Caribou Eskimo shaman who fasted for 30 days in freezing cold, Tiger seems to believe that "the only true wisdom lies far from mankind," as Igjugarjuk put it, "out in the great loneliness, and can only be reached through suffering."

Stories about Tiger's unrelenting discipline abound: how, only one day after winning the 2000 PGA, his third major in a row, Tiger was back on the range for an intense two-hour practice session in the hot sun—but only after going for a seven-mile jog; how he hustled to the range for a lengthy tune-up immediately after a round in which he shot a course-record 61; how he once barked at his swing coach, "Meet me at the range" right after shooting a 63. "Tiger was never satisfied unless he got exactly what he wanted out of every swing," says John Anselmo. "He had to improve on everything he was doing and whatever it took, he would do. I don't even know if he was having fun out there or not. He never showed that he was with me. With Tiger, it was all business, all the time."

And if you think Tiger is goofing off just because he doesn't have a club in his hands, think again. "When he is doing nothing," his mother Tida once told a reporter, "wherever he is, he works on strengthening his palm, fingers and wrist."

Indeed, to the utter dismay of his rivals, Tiger's intention is not to be one of the hardest workers on tour—it is to be *the* hardest worker. "Other golfers may outplay me from time to time," he declared in his book, "but they'll never outwork me." With the possible exception of Vijay Singh, whose lust for hitting range balls is legend, no one spends more time or expends more energy refining their game than Tiger Woods. "That's just one of my deals," he explained matter-of-factly in 2002. "I'm always looking to improve my swing."

Even as a child, Tiger understood that his superior talents made it incumbent on him to work even harder than players with lesser skills. When he was three, a TV reporter asked him how he got so good. "Practice," young Tiger said. How much practice? "About a whole bunch." The better Tiger got, the longer and harder he practiced. "He was always trying to maximize his abilities, but that's what all good golfers do," says his first coach Rudy Duran. "What's amazing is that Tiger displayed that desire and interest in maximizing his abilities when he was five years old. It was unbelievable."

As an adolescent "he would practice night and day, that boy," says John Anselmo. "He was very interested in every phase of the swing and he asked a lot of questions—intelligent questions—about swing mechanics. For instance, Tiger really wanted to get rid of backspin. It really upset him that he would hit a great shot and it would pull back off the green. Eventually he learned to control his irons." In college, Tiger spent endless hours in his dorm room watching videotapes of great golfers like Byron Nelson and Ben Hogan, mining the grainy footage for clues that might help him enhance his own swing. "He is by far the most disciplined athlete I have ever worked with," says his Stanford coach Wally Goodwin. "In California you can get out and practice all year round, and Tiger did. He went out a lot and he really put in the hours. I remember Tiger would practice under any and all conditions. He'd go out there in a downpour and just play."

And even though he was uniquely accomplished when he turned pro in 1996—he was the nation's best collegiate golfer and a three-time U.S. Amateur champion—Tiger "had not really done anything when he played in professional events as an amateur," says Roger Maltbie. "Other amateurs had fared much better and had better records in pro events. Phil Mickelson even won a tournament as an amateur. So there were real questions about Tiger when he turned pro. 'What's he going to do when he gets out here? How will he stack up?'"

Tiger answered those questions in a hurry, not only by winning two of his first seven events but by working to fix the flaws in his game even as he was winning. "He didn't just say, 'I'm going to bring what I have out here and see how it works,'" says Maltbie. "He continually worked on refining his game. Early on he had particular problems with distance control with his short irons, so he worked on controlling the trajectory of his shots. He has always shown an enthusiasm for working on the technical aspects of his swing."

What, exactly, is behind Tiger's uncommon drive to improve? Why is it that the world's best golfer feels compelled to wear out four lob wedges a year practicing? On one level, Tiger is merely following a fundamental precept of Buddhism—indeed, a basic law of the universe. "A man's work, however finished it seems, continues as long as he lives," said Lao Tzu. "To continually hone your gift is to properly respect it; to be complacent with it is to squander a blessing. Anything less than unceasing vigilance will disrupt the natural flowering of your talent, preventing you from maximizing your abilities. Laxity will produce results that are incomplete and unsatisfying." In Buddhism, one cannot achieve enlightenment without constant practice; acquiring true wisdom is a slow and painstaking process. "There is no way for others to do the work and for you to reap the results," the Dalai Lama advises in *How To Practice: The Way to a Meaningful Life.* "You will need to practice these techniques day by day, year by year."

Tiger has long demonstrated a profound understanding of this concept, as well as a willingness to do whatever it takes to get the most out of his golf. "People have no idea how many hours I've put into this game," he said in 2000. "My dad always told me that there are no shortcuts, that you get out of it what you put in, and that if you want to become the best, you're going to have to be willing to pay your dues." Earl Woods deflects the credit, pointing out that his son was always an incredible self-starter. It wasn't Earl who picked his son out of his high chair so he could swing his first club at 10 months old—it was Tiger who hopped down himself. And it wasn't Earl who phoned home from work to set up a practice time with his son—it was young Tiger who memorized his dad's work number before he learned how to count, just so he could call him and pester him to go play. "I never had to ask Tiger to practice, not even once," remembers Earl. "And I never had to ask him to go do his home-work. He just always had it done. Tiger was always totally responsible for his own actions." That said, Earl did instill in his son a sense that practice should be consistent, efficient and fun. "Always work on something specific when you practice," advises Earl. "Always pick out a target so you have something to gauge success and failure by."

Of course, all the lessons in the world would have been useless if Tiger didn't already possess the one thing that is essential to main-taining good discipline—a passion for the thing you are practicing. "I was playing something I loved. No one could take that way from me," Tiger has said of his early days playing golf, during which he was taunted by children who felt the sport was for sissies. "They could make jokes, but in the end, I was doing the thing I loved to do, and I wasn't sure they were doing the same."

Blessed with this passion for playing golf, Tiger could tap a bot-tomless reserve of energy and enthusiasm. As he matured, his devotion to practicing became an integral part of who he was, just as his youthful zeal to be the world's best golfer became nothing less than a mission. "Tiger is definitely on a mission, and he feels it will go away if he does not keep renewing himself and building himself up," says Dr. Jim Loehr. "The way we show that we care about some-thing is by building rituals that insure the necessary energy gets funneled to where it is needed. And if we want to be extraordinary the only way that happens is through this force and focus of energy. It does not happen any other way. As Tiger demonstrates, it is all about the energy dynamics that we bring to what we do."

Distressingly for everyone else, Tiger has no intention of diminishing the amount of energy he devotes to his mission. Even "with the talent that I have to play the game," he has said, "I want to be an overachiever. . . . If I can be an overachiever with what I know I can do with a golf ball, I'll have a pretty good career."

And so Tiger goes about his lonely business, tucking himself at the far ends of ranges and chewing up patch after patch of sod. Win or lose, he sticks to his plan: disregard the hype, hunker down, strive always to improve. "You can never master the game, simple as that," he has said, implying that there will always be room for improvement in his already wondrous play. But where, one might ask, does it all end? How long can the guy keep it up? "I think Tiger is going to have a very difficult time eclipsing the longevity of Jack Nicklaus," says Sid Matthew. "Yes, he has been a warrior. He has been like Uriah the Hittite, on the war campaign all the time. But Tiger is going to go through a lot of things in his life. He's going to have kids, he's going to get hurt, he will eventually bury his parents. He is going to face disappointments about where he is and where he wants to be. And a lot of these things may cause him to lose some of the fire he has in his belly right now. Keeping this up for 24 years is going to be very difficult."

Only time will tell if Tiger will ease up on the throttle. Perhaps at one point he will decide the grind is simply not worth it. Or perhaps he will never stop practicing about a whole bunch. As a teenager playing in the Scottish Open at Carnoustie, Tiger endured a round in winterish cold and whipping winds, only to scurry right to the driving range once his round was done. "He told me he had to recalibrate his swing to play in the windy weather," recalls his father, who dutifully accompanied his son to the practice tee. "I'm sitting on this little seat, trying to block this howling wind with my umbrella, and there's Tiger hitting shot after shot. Suddenly I noticed that he had picked out a target, a fence post at the edge of the range, and he began hitting his shots at this post." First Tiger started a shot 50 yards right and drew it in, next he started it 50 yards left and faded it to his target, then a low draw, then a knock-down fade, then a runner that bounced all the way to the post. Earl, freezing in the 40-mph winds, knew just what he was watching. "I said, 'Tiger, you're out there playing, aren't you?'" says Earl. "And Tiger said, 'Isn't it fun, pop?'"

"Tiger was experiencing the sheer joy of executing while he was learning," Earl says. "He still hasn't lost that joy, and I don't think he ever will."

INTEGRITY:
Never Let Up

"Because projects often come to ruin
Just before completion,
He takes as much care at the end as
He did at the beginning,
And thereby succeeds."
—*The Tao Te Ching*

"I've never given up in my entire life on a golf course. You start going bad,
who cares? You've got to get it back."
—*Tiger Woods*

I T WAS HALEY'S COMET, A BLUE MOON, the Cubs winning the pennant—Tiger Woods four-putted a green. It happened when he was a sophomore at Western High School, playing for the league championship against rival Valencia High. On the last hole, Tiger faced a 30-footer for birdie and only needed two putts for his team to win. He missed the birdie putt, then missed the five-footer coming back. The tap in for bogey would have given his team a tie, but a frustrated Tiger casually swiped at the ball, which lipped out of the cup. Stunned, he finally tapped in for a four-putt double bogey. Western High wound up losing the championship by one stroke. "He was a kid and he did kid things back then once in a while," says his high school coach, Don Crosby. "Afterwards, I didn't talk to him about the four-putt. He was still only one or two over par, and we had another kid who was nine shots over, so you can't pin it all on Tiger. But I certainly don't remember him ever doing something like that again."

That a high school player, even one as accomplished as Tiger, would momentarily lose his focus and make a bonehead play is not remarkable. Plenty of professional players have waved at tap-in putts and missed them. What is remarkable is that Tiger seems to have turned his embarrassing four-putt into an indelible lesson—a reinforcement of his commitment to give every shot his best. "Today, you never see Tiger swatting at a ball backhanded or whacking at a shot in the rough in frustration," says Gary McCord. "There is no sloppiness, absolutely none. There is only full preparation before he gets to the easy part, which is actually hitting the shot."

Indeed, it is difficult to recall a single instance in which Tiger, as a professional, mailed in a shot. Quite the opposite, he is famous for playing with the same intensity and attention to detail regardless of the situation, whether he is vying for a major title or competing in a silly season event in Hawaii. On the links Tiger is absolutely relentless, conceding nothing to difficult courses, accepting no dire situation as fate, yielding not so much as a single stroke to Old Man Par. If there is any golf to be played, Tiger will play it and he will play it head-on—he will complete his task with the same energy and enthusiasm as he began it. "Tiger doesn't know how *not* to try his best on every single shot," says Rudy Duran. "He just doesn't know how to do anything else. So if he's 15 strokes back or 15 strokes in front, doesn't matter. For Tiger, a shot is a shot."

The sport of golf, perhaps like no other, has a way of stripping away pretense and exposing flaws. The casually missed back-tap putt is just a dramatic illustration of a very human trait—the impulse to give up when things don't go our way. Not to flat-out surrender, exactly, but to allow our efforts to slacken—to cease being vigilant when vigilance is most at a premium. This is why Buddhist literature urges us to maintain a consistent level of exertion and attention when going about our tasks. It is nothing less than the key to insuring happy results. "Those who strive earnestly will go beyond death," the Dhammapada tells us. "Those who do not can never come to life." And, "the earnest spiritual aspirant, fearing sloth, advances like fire, burning all his fetters. He will never fall back: he is nearing nirvana." Do not let up, we are warned; approach every action with passion and commitment. Anything less will compound our troubles and make the next hurdle that much harder to surmount. "Meet the difficult while it is still easy," says the *Tao Te Ching*. "Cross the universe one step at a time. The sage understands that everything is difficult, and thus in the end has no difficulties."

Tiger's tenacity in all situations is a wonder to behold. He simply does not allow his position on the leader board to dictate how he approaches his round. Even when Tiger is seemingly out of contention, he refuses to concede and performs as if he were a shot out of the lead. At the 2001 U.S. Open at Southern Hills, Tiger was nine shots behind the leader heading into his final round. No fewer than 23 golfers were ahead of him, meaning that Tiger would have to significantly outplay them all to have any chance of winning. By any objective standard, Tiger was hopelessly out of the running. Besides, Tiger had just won four major championships in a row. The guy clearly wasn't going to make it five—wasn't he entitled to slack off a bit and just coast home in his final round?

Tiger would have none of it. He declined to agree with reporters who felt he had no chance of winning, and talked about putting some pressure on the leaders by playing lights-out golf on Sunday. A few birdies, maybe an eagle or two, and who knows? "Those guys are getting started with their rounds, and if I get three or four more [birdies] coming in . . . ," he said afterwards, trailing off before putting into words how a Tiger charge might have caused the leaders to crumble under pressure. "That's how I was thinking." Playing aggressively on every hole, Tiger dazzled fans by birdying the 642-yard par five fifth hole—the longest par five in golf history. But in the end, he ran out of birdies and holes, finishing in a tie for 12th place. "I played as hard as I could on every shot," he said. "I have no regrets."

Integrity of effort—this mattered more to Tiger than winning or losing. And that is saying something, considering how much winning means to him. What might not be instantly apparent is that such sustained effort, even in a losing cause, can lead to success in future endeavors. The mind and body are programmed to perform at a high level, so that when victory is actually on the line there is less chance of lapsing into sloppy play. The memories you summon when the heat is on will be uniformly good ones; there will also likely be a carry-over of positive energy. At the 2003 Nissan Open at Riviera Country Club, Tiger began the final round tied for 28th—essentially, out of contention. Still, on Sunday he played beautifully, racking up seven birdies and matching the low round of the tournament. "I wanted to go out there today and play good for an entire 18 holes," he explained. "I really did hit some good shots." Tiger finished tied for fifth, but that mattered less than what happened the following week. Buoyed by his final round fireworks at the Nissan and coursing on a river of good feelings rather than frustration, Tiger won the WSG-World Match Play Championship. His good work at Riviera carried over; his integrity of effort paid off. "Anciently the skillful warriors first made themselves invincible and awaited the enemy's moment of vulnerability," Sun Tzu says in *The Art of War.* "That which depends on me, I can do."

No quitting, not for a moment, never—no exceptions. At the 2002 PGA at Hazeltine National, Tiger trailed a brash upstart named Rich Beem by four strokes with five holes to go. Beem's bold eagle on the 12th hole, just before Tiger missed a birdie putt on 13, was, most everyone believed, the final dagger for Tiger. Indeed, he appeared rattled when he badly pulled his next tee shot. But then, walking down the 15th fairway, Tiger turned to his caddie, Steve Williams, and said, "If we birdie in, we'll win the tournament. Let's just suck it up and get it done."

Four birdies in the final four holes of a major championship? A tall order, to say the very least. But then Tiger made an eight-footer for birdie on 15, canned a 10-footer on 16, another 10-footer on 17 and, after a magnificent 7-iron to four feet on the final hole, made his fourth birdie in a row. Only a miraculous, twisting 35-foot birdie putt on 16 allowed Rich Beem to win the PGA and relegate Tiger to a rare second-place finish. "I could have easily just, you know, bagged it in and made pars coming in, who really cares," a disappointed Tiger said after the round. "But that's not the way I play. . . . I'm going to learn from my mistakes, and I'm also going to learn from the way I approached those last four holes." Would Tiger view the 2002 PGA as a squandered opportunity? No, he told reporters, he would not. "I gave it absolutely everything I have," he said. "You know that's the way I play each and every time I tee it up."

This includes events other players call hit-and-giggle golf—end-of-the-season frivolities like the Skins Game, designed more as entertainments than truly competitive tournaments. This distinction is lost on Tiger, who shows up just as dialed in as he is for any major. "Doesn't matter what the prize is or what the competition is," says Bobby Clampett. "Tiger goes out and tries to beat the brains out of these guys. It is not part of his demeanor to do it any other way. He is about winning, and why shouldn't he be?"

At the 2003 Skins Game, Tiger was visibly rankled after a fan clicked a camera in the middle of his backswing. Tiger's ire prompted his caddy Steve Williams to yank the camera away from the fan and toss it in a nearby pond. This was the Skins Game, the most casual of all pro events, and here was Tiger ratcheted up to his usual fever pitch. His reaction earned him rebukes—"let's get real," wrote one critic, "[the Skins Game] isn't serious golf"—but what his critics might not understand is that, with Tiger, there is simply is no other gear. If an event has a winner and a loser, Tiger is going to go full-throttle—count on it. "I remember him shooting a 61 at the Grand Slam one year and being mad about one bad shot he hit," says Jim Huber. "I mean, this guy would clunk himself in the head for making a mistake while playing against his buddy Mark O'Meara for five bucks." By never varying his approach to competitive events, Tiger insures the integrity of his effort each and every time he tees it up.

Still, how does Tiger do it? How does he summon such incredible effort even when events are meaningless or all hope of winning seems lost? How can he maintain such integrity of purpose over such a long and exhausting haul? In fact, Tiger manages to keep the quality of his efforts high by relying on a simple trick—creating goals within goals. During the final round at the Nissan his ultimate goal was to win, but his goal within a goal was to "play good for an entire 18 holes," narrowing the scope of his endeavor (remember: "cross the universe one step at a time") and making it much easier to give maximum effort.

Yet as inspiring as Tiger's tenacity is when he is way behind, it is even more astounding when he is way in front. Amazingly, Tiger refuses to ease up on the gas even when he is winning tournaments by obscene margins, for the same reason that he goes for broke when he is out of the running—to maintain integrity of purpose. "With Jack Nicklaus, he just wanted to win and sometimes he would go into safety mode," says Roger Maltbie. "Winning by three strokes was plenty. But Tiger doesn't view it that way. With Tiger, the hammer stays down. He is out there trying to do his absolute best, and if it adds up to winning by 15 strokes, then that's just great."

Maltbie is referring to one of Tiger's crowning moments—his surreal win at the 2000 U.S. Open at Pebble Beach. Tiger's play was so precise, so assured, that as early as the end of the first round some were saying the championship was his. Indeed, Tiger more or less waltzed to victory, playing completely within himself, consistently widening his lead, establishing himself as one of history's most dominating champions—"pretty much making a mockery of the field," according to Maltbie. But none of that mattered to Tiger as he played the 16th hole on Sunday. Leading the tournament by an insurmountable 15 strokes, he missed the green with his approach shot, chipped on with his third shot and faced a difficult 12-footer for par. The putt could not have mattered less; make it or miss it, Tiger was still going to win the U.S. Open by a historical margin. And yet, to the befuddlement of nearly everyone watching, Tiger began stalking the putt as if he were trailing by one. He read it from every angle, studied its subtle break, gave it his usual forensic scrutiny—gave it *extra* attention. Then Tiger calmly stroked the putt and watched it vanish in the cup. "And then he goes and gives it this fist pump!" marvels Maltbie. "And we're all thinking, 'What was that?' He's winning this thing by 15 strokes!"

Afterwards, Tiger admitted to setting a goal within a goal—no bogeys in his final round on Sunday. "That putt was huge for me," he explained. "The fact that I had a chance to play the final round of the U.S. Open with no bogeys. I knew I had to make that putt." Tiger hardly needed such a goal—it is almost inconceivable that he could have played poorly enough to lose his enormous lead. Yet he set the goal nonetheless, insuring that there would be integrity of effort and purpose. "On the road to success, as you near the attainment of your goal, beware becoming intoxicated with your achievement," warns the I Ching. Tiger does not allow himself to think past the very next shot, even if victory is assured. "He ground that son of a gun right in there and he was so excited when it fell in," remembers his dad Earl of Tiger's par putt on 16. "He had a goal that day and it did not matter that he was way ahead. Even when he is winning by a lot, he is not in a comfort zone and he wants to do better. Tiger always tries his very best."

Nowhere is Tiger's integrity of effort more apparent than in the achievement he may be proudest of—his record number of consecutive cuts made. In pro golf tournaments, scores are added up after two rounds so that the field can be cut roughly in half. The top 70 scores or so qualify golfers to play on the weekend; the bottom half are cut and go home. Only those who make the cut receive any prize money; the rest are out travel and lodging expenses. The number of cuts you make in a row is an excellent barometer of how you are playing—to consistently finish in the money means you are getting the job done regardless of where you play and who you play against. As of the 2004 PGA, the golfer with the second most consecutive cuts—Scott Verplank—had made 25 in a row. Tiger, of course, was first—*with 129 cuts in a row*, spanning nearly six full seasons (he broke Byron Nelson's record—113 in a row—in 2003).

In events important and inconsequential, in stormy weather and in sun, through lucky breaks and extreme misfortune, Tiger went out and did what he had to do—every time. For many golfers out of the running by the middle of the second round, the appeal of a free weekend to fish or barbecue with the family is irresistible, and so the struggle to make the cut is not joined. The extra gear needed to stage a comeback is not summoned. Everyone has an off week now and then, don't they? Where's the shame in a missed cut here and there? These are not questions Tiger Woods ever asks himself. "I do not think I could live myself if I knew that I had dogged it," he once said. "That would just eat at me."

To be sure, there were close calls. At the 2004 Western Open he had to birdie two of the last four holes on Friday to make the cut by a stroke; the next day he carded nine birdies to get back in contention. At the 2003 Deutsche Bank Open he was three over par deep in the second round when he learned the cut would be plus one. He ran off six birdies in the next 11 holes to make the cut and eventually finished only six strokes off the lead. At the 2001 PGA he found out on the 15th tee of his second round that he needed a couple of birdies to make the cut. On the 15th green he had an undulating 50-foot chip for birdie and had his caddy tend the flag as he might for a much shorter putt. Sure enough, Tiger canned the chip and drained a 20-footer for birdie on 16 to make the cut by one.

Most nerve-wracking of all was the 2004 PGA, in which an erratic Tiger needed two birdies over the last six holes of his second round to make the cut. Missing the cut meant Tiger might lose his No. 1 ranking in the world. "I wasn't playing well but I had to keep trying," he explained, and indeed he somehow raised the level of his play, digging out one birdie on the par-5 16th hole before curling in a tricky 20-footer for another on 17. "I think that's the one thing I'm most proud of, that I've never bagged it," Tiger said afterwards.

"You're going to have your bad days . . . you just got to somehow find it within yourself to get it done." Some might say there was magic in those last-minute saves, but Tiger has another word for it: pride. "I take great pride in always giving my best all the time," he said in response to a question about his cut streak. "There were many times I probably should have missed [the cut]. You know the old saying, 'You can't turn a switch on and off, you've got to have it always on.' And that's how I've always played. And that's what shows in my cut streak." Says Roger Maltbie of Tiger's persistence: "A father could tell his son, 'Okay, now watch Tiger—each and every time he hits the balls, he is trying his best.' It is an absolute schematic of what you would want to try and teach a young golfer."

It helps, of course, that Tiger has no doubts whatsoever about what he wants to be—the very best golfer of all time. "If you can figure out what your purpose is and where you want to go, then everything else begins to line up," says performance expert Jim Loehr. "You begin to realize what you have to do to marshal the energy to make it happen." This, then, is the source of Tiger's fiercely burning inner light, the fuel that keeps him motivated—a sureness of who he is and what he stands for, a powerful sense of self. His father Earl Woods calls it coming from truth. "Tiger has always been taught to come from the truth," says Earl. "And in order for your life to work properly, you have to come from truth."

"There's a little known fact about Tiger," Earl goes on. "He gets physically ill when he tells a lie. He actually gets nauseous when he isn't telling the truth. This is why he always tries his best. It's because he always has to be true to himself."

Which is why we probably won't see Tiger four-putting—or throwing up—anytime soon.

NO EXPECTATIONS:
Disregard Limits

"To see beyond boundaries,
To the subtle heart of things,
Dispense with names
With concepts,
With expectations and ambitions and differences."
—The Tao Tè Ching

"Knowing that you never arrive is a wonderful thing because you never say,
'This is my limit.' You never put a limitation on your own abilities."
—Tiger Woods

THIS WAS LIKE CLAPTON PLUCKING HIS FIRST GUITAR. Like Pele kicking his first soccer ball. Like Liberace going wherever the heck he went to find his first candelabra. This was Tiger Woods getting his very first full set of golf clubs. He was five years old on the monumental day when his swing coach Rudy Duran ordered a set of custom-built irons from the Confidence Golf company to replace Tiger's ragtag selection of irons and wedges. Tiger himself picked out the club heads he liked at the Confidence factory. But then—a problem. "Tiger asked me why I hadn't ordered him a one-iron or a two-iron," remembers Duran. "I told him it was because he didn't generate enough club head speed to use those clubs." After all, even most professional golfers don't carry a one-iron—it has the least loft of any iron and is the hardest club to hit well. Tiger quietly accepted Duran's explanation.

But a week later, on the driving range at Heartwell Golf Park, Tiger went to his father's golf bag and calmly took out his dad's Ping Eye2 1-iron. "It wasn't a sawed-off club, it was full-length, so it reached up to his neck," says Duran, who had no idea what Tiger was up to. "He just held it at the end and teed up a few balls and started hitting these perfect 1-iron shots. Striped them. He was showing me he did have enough club head speed. And so the next day I ordered a 1-iron and a 2-iron."

Even as a kid, Tiger knew enough not to accept limits on his abilities. He neither imposed any on himself nor tolerated others imposing them on him. Through the years he has carefully avoided adopting rigid goals or numerical performance targets—instead, he has kept expectations fluid, open-ended, purposefully vague. The reason: Tiger understands that overly-specific goals can become ceilings on performance—can turn into barriers that block him from discovering his true potential. He prefers to believe his potential is boundless, which means he will never accomplish enough to squelch his desire. Never arriving means always striving; no expectations means anything's possible. "There is no number that Tiger is chasing," says David Feherty. "His attention is turned totally inward. He is completely absorbed in the act of doing, not by the result. He's not about shooting a 63, he's on a journey to shooting whatever number he shoots."

Here, Tiger demonstrates a deep appreciation of that fortune-cookie synopsis of Zen thinking—there is no path to happiness, happiness *is* the path. The journey is the reward, not the destination; take care of the golf and the golf will take care of you. Do not become attached to numerical targets or short-term goals, for all they can do is inhibit you from achieving even more. "The wise man strives to no goals," says the Zen poem *Hsin Hsin Ming*, "but the foolish man fetters himself." Tiger, unfettered, focuses not on winning tournaments but on hitting winning shots. Asked if it felt good to win the 2001 Memorial, Tiger replied, "It feels good to play good." His expectation when he swings is not to hit it close, for that is a result; instead, he expects only to make a good swing at the ball. "You'll hear Tiger say that all the time," says Feherty. "He's going to make mistakes and so his goal is, 'I want to notice when it happens and why it happened.' He isn't worried about the ball going in, he's worried about his swing."

This is not to say that Tiger never sets goals. We know he does just that to keep motivated—no bogeys in this round, no three-putts in that round, no bad swings for 18 holes. The difference is that

Tiger's goals are less results-oriented than they are process-oriented. Since he doesn't covet trophies but rather covets the kind of performances that win trophies, Tiger's goals are designed to insure he always plays to the best of his abilities. Instead of fixating on outward targets, "his goals come from within," says his father. "They are his goals and no one else's, and he does not share them with anyone. I have never known, since he was a little boy, what his goals were. All I know is that they are always higher than what everyone else's expectations are."

When Tiger does discuss his goals in public, it is almost always in general terms. You might hear some pros say they'd like to win two tournaments and a major in the next year. Others might aim at finishing in the top five on the money list. But you won't catch Tiger talking about numerical goals. To do so would be to limit himself, since deep down he believes victory is *always* within his grasp. "How many times have I told you this?" he once sighed to reporters. "I expect to go out there and win every tournament I play in . . . that's what I strive to do." Tiger knows full well he won't win every tournament, but that does not stop him from striving to play well enough to do so. His eye is on the process, not the prize. "My long-term goals are private," he said after playing in his first pro event, before grudgingly divulging one very Zen-like goal: "To hit the perfect shot."

That said, there is one numerical target that has always fascinated Tiger: Jack Nicklaus's record of 18 wins in major championships. No other golfer has won more than 13. As a child, Tiger kept a tiny, yellowing newspaper clip about Nicklaus on his bedroom wall, not far from the *Star Wars* poster on his closet door. "I think the greatest record of all," he has said, "is [Nicklaus's] eighteen professional majors." Much later, when Tiger finally made it on tour, he discovered he felt a special connection to his boyhood idol, based on their shared goal of being the best. It is hardly surprising that Tiger picked as his role model a golfer who resisted all limits on what he could do. Most famously, Nicklaus confounded conventional wisdom by winning his sixth Masters title at the age of 46. "If you aspire to greatness, you have to have a clear picture of greatness," Tiger would say. "Jack and I have an understanding of each other just because of the way he plays."

In recent years, however, Tiger has downplayed the importance of Nicklaus's record. "Whether I will ever accomplish it or not, who knows?" he said. "But it's not the driving force in my life. The driving force of my life is to get my game at a level where I'll be able to compete in each and every tournament I tee it up in for the rest of my life." Tiger would never set 19 majors as his goal—he knows that while that would take him past Nicklaus, it would not necessarily get him in the vicinity of his own potential. Who is to say Tiger Woods can't win 20, 25, 30 majors? Today, Nicklaus's 18 majors are only a benchmark along the path to Tiger's own and unknown glory. "If everything goes correct in my career," he said in 2004 in response to a question about breaking Nicklaus's record, "I'd like to be in the 20s."

The challenge, then, is not to meet goals or break records but to glimpse the distant sparkle of our own precious potential. In mythology, miracles represent the limitless power in all humans; they dramatize that we are capable of more than we dare dream. But one of the great students of mythology, Joseph Campbell, insisted it is entirely possible that miracles can actually happen. "Three or four times I've seen what appear to be magical effects occur," he claimed in *The Power of Myth.* "Men and women of power can do things that you wouldn't think possible. We don't really know what the limits of the possible might be." Tiger's father echoes this belief. "Tiger has no limits because there are no limits," says Earl. "There are no limits to the universe, so why should we impose them on ourselves? Believing that there are no limits to what we can do is simply following the law of the universe."

Thus Tiger is not waging battle against his fellow golfers or even against Nicklaus and other guardians of history—Tiger is pitted against himself to see what his own limits are. "If you compete with no one," says the *Tao Te Ching,* "no one can compete with you." Tiger put it this way to the sportswriter Tom Callahan: "My goal remains, hopefully, to be the best. The best ever? Who knows? I hope I will become the best ever. *But the best me—that's a little more important.*" The ceiling set by other golfers is of minimal interest to Tiger; his hope is that his own ceiling exists in rarified air, beyond any targets or threshold we recognize today. "Every time Tiger breaks a record and moves into a category with Snead and Hogan and Nicklaus, he revels in that moment," says Jim Huber, "and that's because he knows each step takes him away from them and towards his own plateau."

Tiger has hurtled towards his own plateau faster than anyone could have fathomed, mocking the expectations of others along the way. Few believed he was mature enough to win the 1997 Masters, yet he was 12 strokes better than the runner-up and became the youngest Masters champ ever. Few thought a golfer could shoot under par in every event he played in for an entire year, but Tiger became the first golfer to do just that in 2000. And winning one event three years is a row is so ridiculously difficult, few even considered the chance that someone might be able to win *three* tournaments three years running. Guess who became the first guy to pull that off? "The thinking has been that there is a theory of compression, that we only have the ability to handle so much pressure before having to let the pressure off," says Sidney Matthew. "If you get six birdies in a row, getting a seventh would create too much pressure and you might blow. So we don't get that seventh birdie. But this compression theory is nonsense, and Tiger proves that." One reason Tiger has never subscribed to such thinking, says Matthew, is that "he has this Buddhist outlook. He does not accept the limits other people put on him."

It has proven an enormous advantage that Tiger was raised to explore, and not ignore, his potential. His parents gave him all the room he needed to discover for himself who he was and what he was made of. "Anyone brought up in an extremely strict, authoritative social situation is unlikely to ever come to the knowledge of himself," believed Joseph Campbell, and certainly Earl and Tida Woods believed that, too. "One of the things I learned from the Woods family is that you don't put limits on your child, either high or low," says Tiger's first coach Rudy Duran. "All they ever told him was to do his best on every shot and what happens is what happens, and we will love you anyway. They gave him their unconditional love and support. That's why you never hear Tiger say he's going to win a tournament, what he says is he's going to do his best."

One way Tiger's parents instilled this value in their son was to allow him to make decisions for himself at a very young age. "That built character and strength from within," explains Earl. "I remember when Tiger was young he wanted to hang out with his friends at night, and he came to me and asked me what his curfew was. And I said, 'I don't know, son, you tell me.'" Tiger, ever thorough, spent three days canvassing his pals to see what their curfews were before confronting his father again. "He told me what he thought his curfew should be, and it was an hour earlier than what I was prepared to give him," says Earl. "But the important thing is that Tiger knew I put the decision-making and responsibility in his hands. A child learns things about himself when you do that."

Empowered by his parent's trust and love, Tiger has always felt free to push boundaries, disregard limits, ignore expectations. The corollary to not putting limits on yourself is not accepting those forced on you by others. "If I tried to live off other people's expectations, I don't think I'd be a very happy guy," he said in 2001. "Challenging yourself to reach another level . . . that, to me, is the thrill of it." Tiger is often asked to count himself out of tournaments when he trails the leaders by several strokes—to put a limit on his ability to rally from way back. But he consistently declines to do so. "Anybody who is within 10 shots of the lead can win it," he insisted to reporters who badgered him about his poor showing at the 2001 U.S. Open. "*It can be done.*" Asked another time to numerically rank his choppy play on a scale of 1 to 10, Tiger demurred. "Scale of 1 to 10?" he said. "Somewhere in there." And when reporters tried to define Tiger's brilliant 2000 season as, perhaps, the peak of his career, Tiger would have none of it. "You know, to be honest with you, I don't think you're ever finished," he said. "As soon as you feel like you're finished, then I guess you are finished, because you've already put a limit on your ability and what you can attain. I don't think that's right."

No limits, no labels, no expectations, no goals—just the journey and nothing more. In our world of camera cell phones and fancy SUVs it's easy to attach ourselves to short-term goals and easy rewards, but these can never truly power us as we struggle to make our way. Indeed, coveting prizes and prestige can only hopelessly limit us in the search for our true potential. Tiger treats limits like a plate of cold broccoli—why should any of us be so quick to stomach them?

Heck, Tiger wouldn't take no for an answer even if it came from the ultimate Top Dog. "If God came down and said, 'Tiger, you can only win one major this year,' which major would it be?" he was asked in 1998. "The way I am," he responded, "I'd argue with Him and say, 'Why can't I have all four?'"

Exactly three years later Tiger won his fourth major in a row.

YIELDING SPIRIT:
Make Necessary Changes

"Moving from knowing to
Not knowing—this is good."
—*The Tao Te Ching*

"I think I will continue to learn how to play this game until the day I die."
—*Tiger Woods*

I T TAKES GUTS TO COMPLETELY OVERHAUL your golf swing, but Tiger Woods did it with the abandon of an infant. It helped, of course, that at the time he *was* an infant.

Tiger was 10 months old and had only recently slid out of his high chair to take his first cuts when, abruptly and without prompting, he decided to radically alter his swing. "When he first came down he was swinging left-handed," says his father Earl, who swings from the right side. "He had been watching me and so he became a perfect mirror image of me. And it took him two weeks to figure out that, 'Hey, Daddy's on the other side.'" What happened next astounded Earl Woods. "In the middle of a swing, Tiger stopped, walked around the other side, set up and changed from a lefty to a righty grip. He went into his little waggle and he hit the ball into the net for the first time right-handed. And that's when I said to myself, 'I have got something special here.'"

Sure, this was the instinctive reaction of a blissfully ignorant child—a baby who didn't know enough to be hesitant about such a drastic swing change. What is truly astounding, though, is that Tiger employs precisely the same mindset today. No matter how well he plays, no matter how many dazzling shots he executes, no matter how many championship trophies he lugs back home every year, Tiger continues to approach the game of golf *as if he knows nothing about it.* For someone so accomplished and universally lauded—someone who has reached the very summit of his sport—Tiger's willingness to essentially overhaul his much-envied swing every few years is, among his many virtues, perhaps the most impressive. In Buddhist terms this is known as hollowing out—emptying your mind so you can absorb new knowledge and insight. "I observe everything," Tiger once told a reporter, "but know nothing."

Tiger wasn't just spouting some dime-store Zen jargon. He would beautifully embody the concept of the yielding spirit in the most controversial and mind-boggling move of his career—his decision to completely revamp his swing right after his historic win at the 1997 Masters. "Here is a 21-year-old kid who wins the Masters by 12 strokes and then turns around and decides to change his swing because he didn't like something about it," marvels Gary McCord. "Now that's pretty unique."

It was not a decision that Tiger took lightly. He had become a professional only seven months earlier. He had won four of his first 15 events, an absolutely stunning debut. He knew that changing his swing would mean winning fewer events, which would trigger speculation that he might not be as good as first imagined. He knew people would second-guess his decision to mess with a good thing. None of that mattered to Tiger Woods. Since he does not hold any hard opinions about himself, he is able to be brutally honest about his swing, making it easier to detect flaws that no one else can see. "It is easy to see the faults of others; we winnow them like chaff," says *The Dhammapada.* "It is hard to see our own; we hide them as a gambler hides a losing draw."

In Tiger's case, his glowing press clips and the world's adulation made it that much easier for him to overlook his weaknesses. Yet Tiger never cluttered his mind with the praise of others; to do so would be to distract himself from the truth about his game. "If I know I have a fault I'll change it," he said in 2001, "and sometimes that's the hardest thing to do." Says Bobby Clampett, "Tiger is able to very realistically view and assess his game. He is extremely honest with himself, and that's an attribute that a lot of players don't have. They'll say, 'Oh, did you see that spike mark on the green that pushed my putt off line?' Well, they actually pushed it. And Tiger will always say, 'I pushed it a little there.' He might even make the putt and say, 'I pushed it and I got a real break there.'"

And so it was that not long after the 1997 Masters—the one where he hit all those soaring drives, majestic long irons and not a single three-putt—that Tiger set about the business of tearing down his swing. Just before the start of the 1997 Western Open, which Tiger also won that year, he allowed *Golf Digest* to photograph his swing with its high-tech, high-speed camera known as the Hulcher. The Hulcher broke down Tiger's 120 mph swing into a series of freeze frames, so that it could be analyzed at every crucial position. Tiger looked at the frames after his Western Open victory and told a *Golf Digest* editor that his swing looked almost perfect. The key word there: almost. By then, Tiger had already done a little swing analysis of his own. In the days after his Masters win he pulled videotapes of the tournament and sat down, by himself, to watch them. Without anyone there to gush about his performance or get in his way, Tiger was able to take a hard look at his swing. Let's just say the words "soaring" and "majestic" did not come to mind. "I didn't see one flaw," he would later say, "I saw about ten."

Tiger quickly phoned his swing coach, Butch Harmon. The call began a journey from which there was no return. What was it, then, that so displeased Tiger in that videotape? What could possibly have been wrong with the swing that produced such spectacular results? Baseball players occasionally make small adjustments to their swings, but very few go for total overhauls. Tennis players, too, tend to stick with the swing they have grooved since childhood. What's more, in golf, overhauling a swing is an especially risky endeavor, inviting, as it does, the loss of trust and confidence. An overhaul that doesn't work will lead inexorably to disaster, as a player presses harder and harder and allows self-doubt to creep in. At Tiger's level, the decision to undo your swing piece by piece and rebuild it from the ground up is practically unheard of. The downside is simply too daunting.

Still, Tiger knew there were serious problems with his swing. The biggest one: he swung too hard. Yes, he was known for his length, power and aggressiveness, but Tiger realized the violence of his swing would not serve him over the long haul. "Every time he hit a pitching wedge, the ground would shake and the ball would shoot out like a six-iron," says his Stanford coach Wally Goodwin. "Tiger would always say, 'I'm going to make my living hitting the ball farther than anyone else.'"

In fact, Tiger's exceptional swing speed—upwards of 120 mph, or 15 mph faster than the average pro—made it hard for him to maintain correct positions throughout the swing. Tiger got away with bad positions and technically flawed swings because of his keen sense of timing: he was able to make miraculous mid-swing corrections to keep his club on line. But this approach could not be counted on, least of all in pressure situations. If his timing was off, Tiger would have problems with controlling the distance of his shots. He realized he had to do something to tighten his swing and give himself more control over his shots. "His swing was actually full of flaws because of its speed and its position on top," says Gary McCord. "It was too dependent on timing, and he had to reroute it on the way down. Still, it took a lot of wherewithal to make these changes right after winning the Masters. He could have been cocky, but he wasn't."

Together with Butch Harmon, Tiger got to work. The first order of business was beefing up his forearms, so he would have the strength he needed to manipulate his club into better positions. Tiger took care of that by packing on 25 pounds of muscle. He and Butch also studied videotapes and photographs of golfing greats like Ben Hogan, whose machine-like swing was ideal but hard to imitate. In this, it helped that Tiger has always been willing to learn from the golfers who came before him. Again, because of his success it would have been easy for Tiger to ignore the examples of history, to think, perhaps, that his superiority made it unnecessary to do his homework. But because of his hollowed-out, childlike mind Tiger has always craved the lessons that legends like Hogan and Sam Snead and Jack Nicklaus can impart. "One thing I've always done is watch and learn from other players," he has said. "I also study videotape to pick up little things. This game is all passed on and we don't really learn anything ourselves."

Then came the hard work—remaking Tiger's swing. Tiger would isolate parts of the swing and practice them over and over, repeating a single movement for 30 minutes at a time, demanding that his muscles commit the movement to memory. "I would get so tired I felt like my arms were going to fall off," he would later say in his book. Tiger combined those isolated moves into a coherent swing, which he then practiced for untold hours on the range, pounding literally thousands of golf balls into the ozone. Progress was difficult to gauge; patience was essential.

Out on the tour, Tiger's game suffered. He would plunge into the first of his so-called slumps, winning only one PGA event in the 19 months between July 1997 and February 1999. The chattering started: what's wrong with Tiger Woods? Why isn't he winning? Will he ever be as good as we think he is? Tiger patiently explained that he was working on a swing change, just as he would do when he next decided to alter his swing, leading to the second of his dips in fortune, in 2003 and 2004. "When you change things, it doesn't happen overnight," he said in 2004. "I've been making baby steps. Slow and steady progress."

Indeed, Tiger kept plugging along, sure in his conviction he could improve his swing. Perhaps more than any other physical act in sports, the golf swing is a most fragile and delicate thing, comprised of dozens of parts and angles, and vulnerable like no other swing of its kind. Its execution depends on pinpoint precision, on the exact synchronization of disparate moves, and slight variances in alignment can lead to disproportionately major mistakes. The baseball and tennis swings are instigated by an oncoming ball and thus are more reaction than action—it is impossible for a clean-up hitter to "think" about hitting a 100 mph fastball, he must simply do it. The opportunity to overthink the swing is eliminated, and technical mistakes can be more easily overcome by force and momentum.

The golfer, on the other hand, stands over a stationary ball and must provide the trigger that starts his swing. He must generate all of the power—none is provided by the speed of the ball. He has hundreds of excruciatingly long seconds before he commits to his swing, making him susceptible to doubts, distractions and harmful second-guesses. To be effective the golf swing must be, in one sense, machine-like—endlessly repeating itself, dependably precise. A golfer must be vigilant about his alignment and his balance, and for this reason Earl Woods taught his son that the swing is nothing less than a metaphor for the way of the universe. "There is no greater truth than the golf swing," says Earl. "Because if it is not executed properly, all sorts of things can happen. The only way to hit a golf ball is to have your clubface be exactly where you want it at the proper time. You must be perfectly aligned. And that is also true of the universe. If you are aligned with the universe, if you understand how it works and don't fight it, then your life will work for you. Good things will happen."

It was while practicing on the range at his home course at Isleworth, in the summer of 1999, that Tiger first felt the synchronicity he had been pursuing for nearly two years. He took a swing with an 8-iron and felt, well, nothing. The components of his swing had gelled into a cohesive whole. No spare parts, no clunky moves. He called his coach Butch Harmon and said, "I think I'm back." At his next tournament, the GTE Byron Nelson, Tiger opened with a round of 61. He would go on to win 10 of his next 14 tournaments, including six in a row. He would win seven of 11 majors, including four in a row. He would enter into perhaps the most sustained period of excellence in the history of his sport, and all because he was honest enough to realistically assess his youthful swing and make the necessary changes. "It shows that what drives Tiger is not so much how he compares to his competition at the moment as how to will be viewed historically," says Roger Maltbie. "He's not just beating the guys who are out there at the time. He has his sight set much higher than that. He has a much bigger picture."

To get that big picture—to see the true reality—we must be willing to admit that we know nothing. And not just once, but as often as necessary. Tiger would alter his swing yet again, leading to another long period of difficult play in 2003 and 2004. This time, his changes seemed even harder to implement; for the first time, Tiger's confidence seemed to ebb. By his own admission he had problems trusting his technique, and often allowed self-doubt to alter his swing even as it was underway. His driving, in particular, proved problematic; in one tournament he missed 13 fairways in a row. He let leads slip from his grip and frittered away chances to charge, things he almost never did during his glory years. The aura of invincibility that surrounded him vanished; his rivals gained so much ground that Tiger became just another top golfer. He lost his No. 1 world ranking, dropping to No. 3. "The shock and awe has kind of worn off a little," says David Feherty. "And the gap has narrowed because these guys were always great and now they're even better. But you know that Tiger will get it together again. And he won't have to say anything when he does. We'll notice."

What Tiger never did was exhibit any ambivalence about his decision to change his swing. Never once did he appear to doubt that the hollowed mind is the one true path to wisdom. If Tiger Woods, paragon of excellence, is willing to yield his expertise and admit he knows nothing, why would anyone else stubbornly cling to fixed opinions about themselves? Is this not one of the most precious lessons Tiger has for us—be like the child who comes to the world with a clean and empty mind? "Allow yourself to yield, and you can stay centered," says the *Tao Te Ching*. "Allow yourself to bend and you will stay straight. Allow yourself to be empty, and you'll get filled up. Allow yourself to be exhausted, and you'll be renewed."

"Having little, you can receive much. Having much, you'll just become confused."

SURENESS:
A Refuge Unto Oneself

"A solid rock cannot be moved by the wind,
The wise are not shaken by praise or blame."
   —The Dhammapada

"My dad once told me, 'No matter what anyone says or writes, really, none
of those people have to hit your little four-foot putt. . . . You have to go do
it yourself.'"
   —Tiger Woods

IS MAJESTY THE KING OF THAILAND, on the occasion of
his birthday, wished to have the company of the most famous
half-Thai athlete in the land. And so it was that Tiger Woods received
the high honor of a personal invitation to meet with the monarch of
his mother's native country. What would young Tiger say to his
esteemed host when the two finally met? As it turned out, Tiger did-
n't say anything to the King at all.

That's because Tiger blew him off.

Well, that's a little harsh. Tiger, in Thailand to play in a tournament, did extend his sincere regrets for not being able to meet with
the King, citing "mandatory contractual appearances" as his excuse.
"I trust you understand," he wrote in a sweet letter of apology, "and
hopefully I will be extended another invitation by the Thai govern-
ment at a later date." Some might view Tiger's regal snubbing as
youthful insouciance, others as the typical hubris of a spoiled superstar. In fact, Tiger was merely doing something he has pretty much
always done—making his own decisions and not much caring what

people think. For most of his life and certainly all his career, Tiger has rigidly kept his own counsel, ceding very few important decisions to his handlers, lawyers, agents or even his parents, and fully accepting the consequences of his actions. He has sought the input of thoughtful people and accepted the advice of teams of professionals, but in the end it is Tiger who calls the shots. It is also Tiger who takes the heat when his decisions rankle someone or prove unpopular, and this he has done with preternatural assurance and no discernible increase in pulse rate. That's because Tiger appears as impervious to criticism as he is oblivious to praise. "You can think what you want about Tiger, it just doesn't concern him," says David Feherty. "And somehow he manages to do that without seeming arrogant. That's not an easy thing to do."

Much of Tiger's insistence on charting his own path through the thicket of his celebrity has to do with the unique demands of his fame. Where is the wisdom in relying on the guidance of others or taking criticism to heart when he is the only person on the planet who truly knows what his life is like? "He has so many issues that he has to deal with, you and I have no clue," says Bobby Clampett. Since Tiger is pulled in so many different directions—by nosy reporters, corporate sponsors, persistent fans and, yes, even by heads of state— he inevitably has to make tough choices to defend what matters most to him: his performance on the golf course. The risk is appearing insensitive, cloistered, unfriendly, but Tiger is okay with that. "He is very comfortable with himself and with the way he thinks and acts," says Jim Huber. "There are some people who might have a problem with that, but how can you knock it?"

Tiger's reliance on his own judgment and disregard for popular opinion are consistent with his Buddhist beliefs. "Favor and disgrace are equally problematic," the *Tao Te Ching* tells us. "Favor lifts you up; disgrace knocks you down. Either one depends on the opinions of others and causes you to depart from your center." Only you can judge your own worthiness, since only you know what is in your heart. Using the opinions of others to gauge your success in life is utter folly. "Raise yourself by your own efforts," the Buddha advised. "Be your own critic. Thus self-reliant and vigilant you will live in joy."

Tiger Woods—like each and every one of us—is the ultimate

guardian of his special gift. The difference is that, unlike many of us, he simply will not be swayed from his beliefs in how best to guard it. This is all the more remarkable considering how Tiger's decisions are dissected and scrutinized not by a handful of busybodies but by a global press. "Everything I do is nitpicked," he told sportswriter Tom Callahan. "That's a tough way to go." Since pleasing all those nit-pickers is impossible, Tiger rightly lowers the volume on them to a harmless din. Life in a fishbowl only works if you ignore the people tapping on the glass.

Tiger's sureness has, at times, left him open to criticism, even from his peers. An example is how he handled the death of the gifted and popular PGA star Payne Stewart. On October 25, 1999, a chartered Lear jet carrying Stewart from Orlando to Houston—site of that week's Tour Championship—veered wildly off course and finally crashed in Aberdeen, South Dakota. Stewart's shocking death at age 42—caused by a rare pressurization failure in the cabin that rendered the two pilots and four passengers unconscious—rocked the PGA and cast a pall over the Houston event. That Sunday 24 players wore plus-fours—the old-fashioned high pant leg that Stewart favored—as a tribute to their fallen friend. Only five players did not, and Tiger Woods was one of them. Still, when Tiger won the tournament—shooting a 67 and 69 on the weekend after flying to Orlando for the funeral on Friday—he raised his crystal trophy in honor of Stewart, one of his closest friends on tour.

The following year, one day before the start of the 2000 U.S. Open at Pebble Beach, Stewart's buddies held a memorial service for him on the 18th green. An early-morning mist off the Pacific Ocean and the plaintive wail of bagpipes made it a beautiful and touching tribute to an unusually vibrant man. But while most of the top players in the world were shedding tears for Stewart, Tiger Woods was out playing golf. Along with Mark O'Meara and John Cook, Tiger skipped the service to get in his customary 6 a.m. practice round. He might have pushed the round back to attend the memorial, but he chose not to do so. Instead he stuck hard and fast to his plan. Afterwards, he was criticized for putting golf ahead of the memory of his friend. Tiger didn't flinch, and anyone waiting for a hint of contrition is still waiting. "I figured I've gone all through it with the [previous] memorial services, and I felt by going, it would be more of a deterrent for me during the tournament, because I don't want to be thinking about what transpired," he explained. "It all depends on how you are personally. If that's how you want to put closure to it, that's how you want to put closure to it. I handle things a little differently."

Tiger unapologetically placed winning above all else, including the memorial that nearly everyone else felt was more important than any tournament. Sure enough, Tiger was spotted practicing on the putting green late into the evening, closing out a full day of preparation for the Open. In fact, says David Feherty, one of Stewart's best friends, skipping the memorial "was *exactly* what Payne would have done. All these guys are out there on the 18th fairway staring out to sea, but Tiger Woods is trying to win the golf tournament. And that is exactly what Payne Stewart would have been doing. Funerals are for the living, they're not for the dead." Bobby Clampett, one of the organizers of the memorial service, does not fault Tiger for not attending. "I wouldn't cast judgment on him," he says. "It is a personal thing." That weekend, Tiger won the U.S. Open by an unprecedented 15 strokes.

The point is not whether it was right or wrong to skip the service, the point is that Tiger did what he believed was best for him, just as all the players who attended were following their hearts. How others would view him did not factor into Tiger's decision. Still, some might ask, where does sureness end and selfishness begin? Isn't Tiger's unbending commitment to all facets of his golf to the exclusion of other legitimate demands just a glorified form of self-absorption? How can skipping a friend's memorial service be considered a virtue?

The truth is that to succeed all athletes must be terrifically self-absorbed and selfish about their time—the competition is just too fierce for them to give less than 100 percent. What's more, we sports fan demand that our heroes be totally devoted to their tasks, and we scream and holler when we detect the slightest diminution of effort. We *want* professional athletes to be selfish—we're not paying top dollar to watch some weekend softball league. Now, if you want to say that Tiger takes being self-absorbed to a wild extreme, you would be right to say it. But that is precisely why he has been so successful; he takes *everything* to an extreme, as long as it helps him win.

And so, while most of us sometimes do things just "for appearance's sake," Tiger doesn't waste much time worrying about appearances. His personal goals are so stratospheric he simply cannot afford to deviate from his plan to please or impress people. Were Tiger only interested in hording trophies and not in helping others through the example of his play and his Tiger Woods Foundation, it might be fair to view him as self-centered—which is just how many fans view baseball's best player, the surly Barry Bonds. But Tiger is intent on having more of an impact on the world than any athlete before him, and to do that he knows he must first take care of business on the golf course. If that means being perceived as arrogant and untouchable, so be it. "Tiger does not have the approachability that he once had, but that's normal," says David Feherty. "If he's walking through a lobby and makes eye contact with some one, the next thing you know he's surrounded. And some people will confuse what he's doing with arrogance, but really he's just looking out for himself. It's just a matter of survival."

How, then, do we go about releasing attachment to other people's opinions? How do we develop this imperviousness to criticism and sureness of character? In Tiger's case, the advantage once again was the way his parents brought him up. From very early on he was encouraged to make his own decisions and, just as importantly, to stand by them. "They have raised me well," Tiger told the world in his first press conference as a professional. "They have taught me to accept full responsibility for all aspects of my life." Earl Woods went against the grain in his approach to parenting, choosing to be more of a friend to young Tiger and less of an authority figure. "The attitude I adopted about our relationship was that we were equals," says Earl. "I never talked down to Tiger. I never had a selective vocabulary with him. I always spoke to him as an adult, and he understood that."

Accustomed to making decisions from an early age—as a teen he'd book hotels for himself and his dad when they traveled to tournaments—Tiger developed a confidence in his own judgment. "He was not a guy who was very easily swayed, even back then," says his college coach, Wally Goodwin. "He just wasn't impressionable. He had a lot of fun with the guys on the team but he always did his own thing. He was methodical about it. When he didn't go to Payne Stewart's memorial, he was just reacting the way he always has. This is the way Tiger lives his life."

When he turned pro, Tiger's sureness didn't always sit well with players or reporters. As a rookie he pulled out of the Fred Haskins Award dinner at the last minute, despite being that year's honoree.

Tiger's excuse? He was worn out by the grind of his first few weeks on tour. Several pros jumped on Tiger for skipping the time-honored function, and for perhaps the last time Tiger seemed stung by the criticism. "I thought those people were my friends," he would say. The dinner was rescheduled to accommodate him, and at the podium Tiger said, "I admit I was wrong" not to attend the first time around. Even so, Tiger's decision to take a week off and rest—inconceivable to some, considering that Tiger was a peppy 20 years old—wound up paying off. The very next week a refreshed Tiger won the Las Vegas International.

As a 19-year-old amateur playing in the Masters, Tiger blew past a group of reporters waiting to interview him after a practice round. He did so even as veteran players were stopping to chat with the media. A *USA Today* article criticized Tiger, but he later explained that his plan was to avoid the press except for a scheduled news conference. "That's the rules this week," he said with the assuredness of a much older player, "to make it easier for me." Athletes like Tiger, says Gary McCord, "are going to march to their own beat and do what they want to do. And they know the press will follow." To be sure, as his career progressed—and at the urging of his coach Butch Harmon—Tiger became considerably more accommodating to the media.

For the most part, though, it is Tiger's life, Tiger's rules. When President Bill Clinton invited him to an event honoring baseball great Jackie Robinson, Tiger surprised everyone by turning him down. It later became clear that Tiger was not interested in generating publicity for politicians of either stripe (Tiger would later privately call Robinson's widow to tell her how much he respected and idolized Robinson). In 2002, he was singled out by women's groups demanding he boycott the Masters until Augusta National changed its male-only admissions policy; that same year the NAACP wanted him to boycott events in states that still flew the Confederate flag. Tiger declined to help both times. "People are always trying to pigeonhole me into a champion of all causes," he would say. "That's not fair."

Tiger has often been called on to identify himself as an African-American, but Tiger—equally proud of his Asian heritage—has never taken the bait. "I'm not out just to be the best black player," he said. "I want to be the best *golfer* ever." Some people feel Tiger plays too few events each year—indeed, 2003's top money earner, Vijay Singh, edged out Tiger for that honor but had to play in *eight* more tournaments to do it. Unfazed, Tiger draws up his schedule early in the year and rarely deviates from it, playing in only a select few events so he can focus his energies on the majors.

Another example: for years Tiger was one of the only golfers to resist the lure of new club technology. While most fellow pros signed up for bigger and better club heads and more advanced graphite shafts, Tiger stuck with his trusty clubs, which were themselves patterned after those used by his idol Jack Nicklaus more than two decades earlier. "I haven't fully taken advantage of the new technology," he would say. "I haven't gone to graphite. I haven't lengthened any of my shafts . . . nothing has really changed in my bag. I just really have improved my technique." (Recently, Tiger did upgrade his equipment and go with longer, lighter clubs, years after nearly all of his rivals did).

Yet the pressure to try new equipment was nothing compared to the clamor for Tiger to re-team with Butch Harmon, the fabled swing coach who helped shape him into the world's best player. The two parted company after Tiger's four consecutive majors, and since then Tiger has not been as accomplished a player. The world, it seems, is convinced Tiger could regain his dominance if only he would eat a little crow and dial up his old coach. But Tiger consistently shrugs off the idea. "As far as asking for help with my golf swing, no," he said in 2004. "But friendship-wise, yes. Butch will always be my friend, and hopefully I will always be his." The reason Tiger fired Harmon after experiencing so much success with him? It was simply time to go it alone, said Tiger, calling himself "very individualistic."

Clearly Tiger has grown an extra skin to protect himself from criticism, so immune is he to the slings and arrows of outrageous pundits. He has said he feels most criticism of him is "very bi-polar" and "unfair," and thus unworthy of his attention. What's amazing is that Tiger has an equally low regard for the *nice* things people say about him. Just as he cannot be toppled by harsh sentiment, he refuses to be bolstered by lavish praise. "Some of the good shots I hit weren't as great as you guys made them out to be," he once said, "and the poor shots weren't as poor as you said. When I win, it's, 'Oh, he can never lose.' And then I don't win a couple and it's, 'Are you in a slump?'" In 2001, not long after winning three straight tournaments and his fourth major in a row to quiet talk of a slump, Tiger took the media to task for its flip-flop analysis of his game. "They make more of it when you are playing well and they make more of it when you are playing bad," he said. "That's just the way it is."

That, however, is decidedly *not* how it is in the world of Tiger Woods. He does not court the approval of others (except, perhaps, for his parents) nor is he crushed like a soda can when he is second-guessed. To succeed at the level that he has, under the pressure of more positive *and* negative scrutiny than any athlete in history has endured, Tiger has had to make his own rules, and not follow those rendered obsolete by his brilliance. In this regard, his sureness has served him like a force field, deflecting carps and hype with equally efficiency.

Wouldn't any one of us benefit from developing a similar indifference to outside opinion? Should we not aspire to a Tiger-like sureness? There will be times in all our lives when we have to make unpopular decisions, and as a result be subjected to the unflattering judgment of others. But as long as we believe what we are doing is right, we will have nothing to apologize for. For, as Tiger knows, the only judgment that really matters is that which we pass on ourselves.

"Be ye lamps unto yourselves," the Buddha advised. "Look not for a refuge in anyone besides yourselves." Those who heed the call of their own hearts, said the Buddha, "shall reach the very topmost Height."

VISION:
Think the Unthinkable

"Out of silent subtle mystery
emerge images . . . thus do all things
emerge and expand out of darkness."
—The Tao Te Ching

"My creative mind is my greatest weapon . . . a kind of inner vision that
enables me to see things others might not."
—Tiger Woods

THIS WAS THE CHALLENGE: hit a shot at least 110 yards to get it over a pond. This was the problem: Tiger Woods' best shot would only go *100* yards. Tiger, a runty six years old, was playing in an exhibition match with his coach Rudy Duran at the Chalk Mountain golf course when they arrived at the 12th hole, a 194-yard par 3 with a creek 100 yards from the tee and a cart path spanning the creek. Duran hit first and wound up just off the green. Then came Tiger. "I knew he wanted to get over the creek but he couldn't hit it far enough to do it," says Duran. "I thought he would have to lay up short of the water."

Which is why he was surprised when Tiger reached into his bag and pulled out his driver. Duran held his tongue. "I figured maybe he's going to take a shorter swing, take a little speed off it, hit it short," he recalls. "But he didn't, he just ripped it." Duran watched in wonder as Tiger's ball landed in front of the creek, bounced across the cart path and wound up 50 yards short of the green. "I looked at him and said, 'Boy, that was lucky,' because I thought he accidentally hit it too far. And he looked at me and smiled and said, 'That wasn't luck, that was what I was trying to do.'" Tiger chipped up and two-putted for a four. Duran got a five.

How could it be that a boy of six was able to envision a shot a crafty veteran like Duran could not see? Was Tiger demonstrating precocious golf vision when he found a way to carry the creek or was he just a kid playing with devil-may-care abandon? In fact, "the shot Tiger took was well within his capabilities," says Duran. "The cart path wasn't one foot wide, it was a good 10 or 12 feet wide. It was a reasonable risk/reward shot." Still, how many six year olds— heck, how many *thirty-six-year-olds*—would not only have thought to put the cart path into play but then also perfectly executed the shot? "To knock a ball on a cart path when you're six? *Hello?*" says Duran. "It shows great imagination and feel, which Tiger continues to show. So am I surprised to see the shots he hits today? No, because I've seen him do it countless times before."

Thus Tiger proves that genius sometimes lies not in the execution of a shot but in its fathoming. And when it comes to creating golf shots where none were thought to exist—when it comes to thinking the unthinkable—Tiger simply has no peer. "He can see shots that no one else can envision—that I couldn't envision in my wildest dreams," says Gary McCord. "I could sit around for hours and not come up with what he comes up with. He has hit a million shots like that." Ernie Els, the victim of more than one of those shots, marveled at Tiger's uncanny on-course vision in 2000. "Tiger sees things differently," he said after a season in which he finished second to Tiger in several events. "He sees the line—not just of his putts, on all his shots—more clearly. I'd like to know how he does it. He might not know himself."

Part of the reason Tiger is golf's leading visionary is that he is also the sport's most impressive physical specimen. That he can twist himself into a pretzel to dig a ball out of foot-high rough or crank his swing up to 140 mph to sail a ball over 30-foot trees—contortionists' tricks few PGA pros can perform—quite naturally means he'll be able to envision more shots than the average player. More weapons at your disposal means more options on the battlefield. Yet Tiger's talent for pulling off difficult shots is one thing. His ability to pull off *impossible* shots is quite another. Tiger routinely envisions shots that didn't even *occur* to observers; he produces trajectories, distances and directions that are beyond the comprehension of seasoned analysts. "He's like the guy in the *Terminator;* he morphs into whatever golfer he needs to be to make a shot," says David Feherty. "Part of my job is to be able to predict what any given player is liable to do in any given situation. And then Tiger comes along and I'm totally unqualified. When he hits these shots I'll be standing there and just want to throw away my microphone. What's the point? Shots that were previously inconceivable, he pulls off."

Exhibit A: the legend of his second shot on the par four 15th hole at Torrey Pines, in the final round of the 2003 Buick Invitational. Tiger pushed his tee shot into long, chewy rough behind a large tree—an indisputably doomed lie. Even if he could manage to get the ball out of the thick rough and under the low branches in front of him, he still had a steep bunker between him and the green, nearly 200 yards away. David Feherty, walking alongside Tiger that day, studied the lie before Tiger hit and felt all hope was lost. "I rely on David's expertise and he said Tiger's only shot is to trap it under the branches and try to run it up somewhere in front of the green," says Bobby Clampett, who called the action from a TV tower. "Then we just stood back and watched."

Nobody saw it coming. None of the savvy analysts had the slightest inkling. No one even considered the possibility that Tiger might go for the green. All they saw was a sadistic lie—a surrender situation. Tiger saw something else. "He hits this six iron that starts low to go under the branches and then shoots straight up in the air, out of this bad lie, and flies 197 yards," says Clampett, "and it stops on a dime 12 feet from the hole. And you sit there and you say, 'Now wait a second.' And I hear David say, 'Oh, come on, I quit.'"

Gary McCord remembers that "first Tiger had to bullet it under the branches, then he had turn it up in the air, and then he had to really swing it from right to left because he had a cross bunker to the right of the pin, and then the ball lands on the green like a bean bag. You put yourself in that position and you say, 'How would I react?' and when I went out afterwards to look at that lie I knew I would have chipped it out. It's hard to convey in simple words what kind of shot that was. It is not possible to hit that shot, *and yet Tiger hit it.*"

Feherty calls Tiger's sliding/sailing/hooking blast out of the spinach "maybe the most remarkable shot I've ever seen. I'm not stupid enough to say things like, 'Tiger can't do this' or 'He won't try that' anymore. I may think those things, but I sure don't say them on the air."

Inventive shot-making has been a staple of Tiger's game from very early on, and those who pay close attention to his play learn quickly to suspend disbelief. "You cannot imagine some of the shots he hit when he needed to hit them," says one of his first coaches, John Anselmo. "The most unbelievable shots, and he hit them all the time." That is because, for Tiger, creating pathways through the clutter of obstacles is what life is all about. Because of both his mother's Buddhist teachings and his father's exhortations to go with the flow of the universe, Tiger has been trained to look beyond hazards and distractions to see true reality, both on and off the golf course. It is apparent that Tiger possesses an unusually vivid mind, strong enough to visualize ways around barriers that appear impenetrable. Can't go through a brick wall? How about going over? Tunneling under? Tearing it down brick by brick? That sort of dogged thinking is Tiger's default mindset.

Consider that two people staring down the same fairway don't always see the same things; some can't stop looking at the trees, bunkers and rough, others see only a shimmering patch of green. Tiger knows the hazards were put there *precisely* to lure his mind away from its proper thinking—that they are not to truth of the hole but rather its trappings. Thus it is incumbent on him to find that truth, to keep his mind fixed firmly on what *can be* and not on what *is now*. "Recognize that everything you see and think is a falsehood, an illusion, a veil over the truth," Lao Tzu teaches us. "Peel all the veils away and you will arrive at the Oneness."

This brings to mind the Zen koan about the hundred-foot pole. A Zen master once asked another teacher, "How can you proceed on further from the top of a hundred-foot pole?" The older, wiser teacher replied, "You, who sit on top of a hundred-foot pole, although you have entered the Way you are not yet genuine." The next step to true enlightenment? "Proceed on from the top of the pole."

Well, you might ask, how exactly does one proceed from the top of a hundred-foot pole? The first thing you have to do is throw logic away. Koans—Chinese for "cases"—are unsolvable riddles Zen masters designed for their students to encourage them to see past boundaries and conceive the inconceivable. Koans are meant to awaken us to the true experience of life—to free us from our perceptions of or expectations about that experience. This is why the master sitting atop a hundred-foot pole is gently urged to contemplate going on further from there. It is through that contemplation of an impossible situation that the master frees his mind. You go further by considering how to go further—the answer to the puzzle is the puzzle itself. Thinking the unthinkable exercises the imagination and expands the boundaries of the mind. In this way, you can liberate yourself from the limits others impose on you and the limits you set for yourself. The new parameters of your mindset allow you to "go further" in your life.

It is not known whether Tiger Woods ever sat atop a hundred-foot pole. But we do know that he once stood in a deep and frightening chasm. Actually it was a fairway bunker on the 18th hole of the Glen Abbey Golf Club in Oakville, Ontario, where he was winning by one shot going to the final hole of the 2000 Canadian Open. Trailing him was the hottest golfer on the course, Grant Waite, who was paired with Tiger that day. Waite hit his tee shot on 18 and found the fairway; Tiger pushed his and plunked it in the long bunker to the right. Hitting first, Waite put his second shot on the green, 25 feet to the left of a pin tucked way right and impossibly close to the giant pond fronting the green. His nifty approach gave him a great shot at two-putting for a birdie that would tie Woods. To win, Tiger would have to get a birdie of his own.

Unfortunately, Tiger's ball was in the bunker 218 yards from the flag. To get it anywhere on the green he would have to pick it cleanly out of the clumpy sand, bore it through the late-evening wind, carry it over a stand of interfering trees, sail it over the enormous pond and somehow keep it from tumbling over the green and into more hazards. Some figured that Tiger, ever daring, might attempt a heroic shot and try to land the ball somewhere on the green—safely left, to be sure, around the spot that Waite aimed at. Others suspected that even the magnificent Tiger Woods would have to show respect for the difficulty of the shot and chip out short of the green, thus taking the water out of play. No one even entertained the possibility that Tiger would try and hit it close to the flag, as a way to guarantee his birdie and the win. Aiming at the flag was just too risky—actually, flat-out dumb—since coming up even a little short meant finding the water and losing the championship. In golf terms, it was utterly incomprehensible.

Even so, Tiger unsheathed his six iron, settled into his customary pre-shot routine, gathered himself against the elements and slashed mightily at his golf ball. It sprung out of the bunker and over the trees and hung above the water for an eternity, prompting one TV commentator to utter, "Oh, no." But then the ball kept going, further and further, until it began its soft descent, floating back to earth and landing, finally, just past the flag. When it stopped rolling it was only 18 feet from the pin. No one had seen it coming; no one had fathomed Tiger's path. Naturally he got his birdie and the win. "He's like a Zen master," the gallant Grant Waite later told *Sports Illustrated.* "He plays every shot fully committed and without fear. He's not going to allow anything—an opponent, a noise from the crowd, the difficulty of the shot—to interfere with his effort to execute the shot . . . that's the essence of golf." Says Bobby Clampett, "Tiger had 200 yards and the worst possible angle from the right bunker. There's a place that everybody would play that shot and that's 30 yards left of the flag. The most courageous shot would be to the middle of the green. But Tiger wasn't even thinking that! I mean, come on! Nobody in history would have the strength and vision to hit a shot like that."

Developing the physical strength needed for challenging shots takes time, hard work and know-how. The same is true for beefing up what Tiger calls the "inner vision." Peeling away the layers of deception one by one—first the bunker, then the trees, then the wind, then the water—is strenuous work and not for the faint of mind. But it can be done, and anyone can do it. Professional athletes, in particular, work hard on improving their visualization techniques, so that they can imagine the shot they want to hit or the pass they want to throw or the race they want to run before they actually do it. "If an athlete can picture in advance each movement of an event exactly as it should be, in a relaxed meditative state, the greater the chances will be that he or she will carry out those movements during the actual performance," say Chungliang Al Huang and Jerry Lynch in *Thinking Body, Dancing Mind.* Put simply, negative images that form in the brain—of a bunker or a pond—block the mind from going further to find a solution. You cannot think past them; like the guy on top of a hundred-foot pole, all you can visualize is the fall. Replacing those negative images with positive ones—a welcoming green, unobstructed by hazards—facilitates bold and creative play. Ignoring the hundred-foot drop allows you to fly with the birds or skip on the clouds.

The key to making such visualization work, say Al Huang and Lynch, is practicing it until it becomes a habit. Tiger did not come upon his ball in the bunker and, out of the blue, dream up a risky shot he could play; he had already spent countless hours training himself to think inventively. Tiger can often be spotted staring down fairways for long minutes before a shot, oblivious to everything but the palette for his next masterpiece. Watch him in these moments of intense visualization and you can almost feel the hazards dropping out of his field of view. Tiger's mental conditioning allows him to carve a path for his ball that is neither unrealistic nor improbable— just beyond the ability of most other minds to grasp. "Tiger has positive feelings about what he can do, and he doesn't let negativity enter into it," says his father Earl. "Think how much more that makes possible in your life. You just have to realize that everything is possible, and everything is possible *right now.*"

We may never be able to accept that everything is possible, but thanks to Tiger Woods we know that much more is possible than we had previously believed. Perhaps we have a better appreciation of the extraordinary power of the mind. In this way, Tiger serves as our inspiration, our role model; indeed, our hero. For what are we doing when we tell and retell the stories of Tiger's amazing feats but mythologizing him? And isn't he doing exactly what the heroes of myth did—showing us a path through the dark and frightening forest? We still speak with reverence of Gene Sarazin's double eagle and Arnold Palmer's driven green and Jack Nicklaus's laser one-iron that stung the flag on 17 at Pebble Beach. Surely we will still speak of Tiger's bunker shot at Glen Abbey 50 or 100 years from now. That's because such heroics touch us in a tender spot—our fragile belief that we, too, have greatness within. "Myths grab you somewhere down inside," Joseph Campbell observed in *The Power of Myth*. "Myths inspire the realization of the possibility of your perfection, the full-ness of your strength, and the bringing of solar light into the world. Slaying monsters is slaying the dark things . . . but if you think, 'Oh, no, I couldn't do that,' that's the dragon locking you in."

Thus Tiger's slaying of monstrous holes makes him a hero—but only if we follow his example. The most heartening aspect of his mental prowess is that there is nothing magical or supernatural about it. He does not have special X-Ray vision nor can he bend a lob wedge with his mind. Like everything else in Tiger's game, his ability to envision spectacular shots has its roots in practice, diligence and sacrifice. Basically, it's grunt work, something all of us can do. The results, though, are most certainly magical. "To be able to pull off some certain shots that...you look back in hindsight and you wonder, 'How did I do that?'" Tiger once remarked. "It felt so easy at the time. You drop the same ball there with nobody around and you try to do it again, it would be a lot harder to do."

And so we keep watching, to see Tiger traverse oceans and reroute bullets and bounce golf balls on cart paths that to us are just places to walk. What fun it all is, unless it's your job to put the inconceivable into plain English. "I kidded with Tiger one time, I said, 'You know, you're going to get me fired,'" says golf analyst Roger Maltbie. "Tiger said, 'How's that?' And I said, 'One day you're going to hit one of those impossible shots that only you can hit, and I'm going to say, 'What the #@%*@! was that???' And those will be the last words I ever utter on air."

Not quite a Zen koan, but we get the point.

ADAPTABILITY:
Clarity in Chaos

*"If your mind becomes firm like a rock
And no longer shakes
In a world where everything is shaking
Your mind will be your greatest friend
And suffering will not come your way."*
    —From The Theragatha, the early Buddhist songs

*"I like the feeling of trying my hardest under pressure. It's so intense some-
times, it's hard to breathe. It feels like a lion is tearing at my heart."*
    —Tiger Woods

I T WAS THE MOST ADVERSARIAL SITUATION Tiger Woods
ever faced, and there wasn't a flag or fairway in sight. He had just
returned to the Stanford campus after attending an awards dinner and
was getting out of his car when a stranger came his way. The man
stuck out his hand and flashed a knife. "Hey Tiger," he said. "Give me
everything you've got." Tiger surrendered a watch and a pendant but
had to explain he didn't carry a wallet. That's when the mugger hit
him in the face with the knife handle and took off. "I went down to
his dorm a little later and I saw a big lump on his jaw," remembers his
Stanford golf coach, Wally Goodwin. "But Tiger only had two
thoughts. One was, 'Gee, that guy could have been caught.' And the
other one was, 'Well, at least he straightened out my overbite.'"

Cool under pressure and incapable of panic—that is Tiger
Woods. He has, in his brief career, shown a remarkable and consistent
ability to turn negative situations into positive ones. He has demonstrated fierce resolve in the face of adversity and an almost sure-fire
penchant for bouncing back after bad shots or unlucky breaks. When

the world around him swirls into chaos, Tiger not only refuses to knuckle under but also somehow manages to elevate his game. Time and again he has thrived in the crucible of pressure-packed final rounds, claiming victory because he was inevitably the calmest warrior. "In the heat of battle, great champions don't get nervous, they get excited," says Bobby Clampett. "They just manage to take their games to a different dimension."

Tiger's seeming imperviousness to pressure is the hallmark of most great athletes. Their ability to perform at their best when the stakes are highest is what sets them apart from lesser players. Indeed, you'll often hear champions talk about how reality seemed to unfold in slow motion when the action was at its most frenzied, allowing them to calmly execute the decisive play. Without this ability to remain calm under pressure—to, as Tiger does, maintain clarity in chaos—a player is likely to succumb to anxiety, his brittle nerves and tightened muscles precluding peak performance. There may be no greater mark of a champion, then, than this mysterious composure in the most hectic moments. "In the tumult and uproar the battle seems chaotic, but there is no disorder," Sun Tzu notes in *The Art of War.* "The troops appear to be milling about in circles but cannot be defeated."

Different champions, of course, slip into this ultra-serene state in different ways. When the heat was on, Larry Bird, the great Boston Celtic, would picture his elderly grandmother—who didn't care for basketball and never watched him play—and think, "I wonder what she's doing right now?" That little trick helped defuse excruciating pressure. With Tiger, something else is at work. He does not divert his focus from the situation at hand; instead he tries to sees the truth of it more clearly. "When the pressure intensifies it seems to have a calming effect on him," says his first coach, Rudy Duran. "He appears to be improving his level of concentration but I think that what we're seeing is the *same* level of concentration that he gives every shot. So his effort is not really volatile, it's just that he is able to give you his best effort when others would crumble like accordions." That may be, but it sure does look like Tiger plays even *better* under pressure. "When he was only seven or so I told him, 'Son, you are one of those special athletes like Larry Bird and Magic Johnson who have this extra gear they can go to anytime they want,'" says Earl Woods. "I told him, 'This is a gift, and you must never forget that you have it.'"

Tiger needed just such an extra gear at the inaugural American Express Championship, contested on the Robert Trent Jones-designed Valderrama golf course in Spain. In the final round, Tiger led a stellar field by two strokes as he prepared to play his third shot on the devilish par five 17th hole. With the title seemingly in his pocket, he had only 100 yards into the green, which was sloped severely back to front and mowed to an ungodly sheen. Its slickness had irritated players all week by introducing the possibility that even well-hit shots could trickle backwards into a pond fronting the green. Sure enough, Tiger struck his nine-iron beautifully, keeping it low and lessening its spin. The crowd cheered when it landed safely 20 feet past the pin and appeared to stop. Even Tiger allowed himself a rare high-five with his caddy. But then—gasps. The ball began to trickle down the green, picking up speed as it tumbled past the flag. In just a few painful seconds it hit the water with a gurgle and sank into its depths.

In the fairway, Tiger stoically watched his shot—and his lead—disappear. He wound up with a triple bogey, dropping him a shot behind hometown favorite Miguel Angel Jimenez, playing a group behind him. The immense misfortune of hitting a perfect shot and still being penalized could have undermined Tiger by triggering a bout of self-pity. But Tiger stood on the tee of the very long and difficult par-four 18th hole and let go of any shock and anger he might have felt. "My only thought," he would later say, "was to make a three." Demonstrating intense focus and resolve, Tiger gutted out a very noble par. When Jimenez bogeyed 18, Tiger had new life. With floodlights fighting off the fall of night, Spanish Civil Guardsmen lining the fairway and an entire nation holding its breath to see if its native son could win, Tiger roped another perfect drive on the 18th hole, on the way to another courageous par. Jimenez could do no better then bogey. Tiger was the champion, having resisted not only Jimenez but also the potentially crushing impact of adversity. "I don't think I've ever seen Tiger play a hole where what happened on the previous hole carried over," says David Feherty. "The 17th at Valderamma is a perfect example of that."

Stepping calmly out of the smoldering wreckage of his triple bogey to manufacture a brilliant and necessary par, Tiger personified a true champion's virtue: the ability to adapt to drastically changing situations. In sports, fortunes can turn on a dime; momentum switches sides with whiplash speed. The champion is the one who best absorbs the dynamics of the change and—sometimes in the span of mere seconds—devises the best response. "As water has no constant form, there are in war no constant conditions," Sun Tzu tells us in *The Art of War*. "Thus, one able to gain the victory by modifying his tactics in accordance with the enemy situation may be said to be divine."

Thanks to the wisdom of both his parents, Tiger learned early on to embrace change. He was taught to understand the fluid nature of sports—indeed, of life—and to go with the flow rather than to desperately thrash about. His mother's Buddhist teachings encouraged Tiger to remain sure and strong in adverse situations—to believe he was better equipped than most to keep cool in pressure spots. "He has an inner peace," Tida Woods told the *Bangkok Post* in 1997. "Sure, he gets mad when he makes a bad shot, but he soon lets it go and is calm again." It is the essence of a Buddha mind to stay centered when the world around you is in turmoil. "Clarity is learned by being patient in the presence of chaos," says Lao Tzu. "Tolerating disarray, remaining at rest, gradually one learns to allow muddy waters to settle and proper responses to reveal themselves."

Earl Woods induced his own brand of chaos as a way to give his son a psychological edge. He purposefully distracted Tiger during practice rounds and imposed only one rule: Tiger could not speak no matter how intense Earl's tactics became. Dropped golf bags, jiggled change, loud coughs and other dirty tricks—all in the middle of Tiger's swing—could be met with only one word: "enough," the safety word Tiger was given to call things off. No whining, no whimpering, no weak excuses—just bearing down, blocking out distractions and business as usual. That imposed silence taught Tiger the only adequate response to adversity is concentrating harder and getting the job done. The mental toughness he developed was, Tiger has said, his father's second gift to him, after the bounty of his physical abilities. "Tiger has this confidence in himself that was built up through experiential things throughout his entire life," says Earl. "He realizes that down the stretch, when it's crunch time, he *owns* crunch time."

Tiger had another important advantage. While most golfers do not experience the crush of fame and media attention until they are professionals, Tiger literally grew up under camera lights. At age two he was in a putting contest with Bob Hope on TV. "I didn't know any different," he has said of his early celebrity. "All I was interested in was going out and playing golf and watching cartoons." Distractions that other golfers might not be accustomed to—swarming galleries, hustling cameramen, the pressure to perform on cue—became second nature to Tiger.

His early golf coach John Anselmo remembers that when Tiger was 11, ESPN asked to tape a segment on him. "They wanted to watch him hit sand shots, so we threw some balls in the bunker," says Anselmo. "The first one Tiger hits, he holes. The second one he hits, he holes too." Unfortunately, the camera wasn't rolling yet. When it finally did, young Tiger had to try and hit another top-notch shot under ESPN's unblinking stare. That sort of pressure could have easily rattled him, but, says Anselmo, Tiger hardly seemed to care. "When they finally turned the camera on and told him go ahead, Tiger hits another one and this time it doesn't go in," he says. "This time it lipped out."

Chaos theory holds that there is order and meaning, maybe even beauty, in seemingly random events. The golf of Tiger Woods proves this theory to be true. In every one of his unprecedented three straight U.S. Amateur Championships, Tiger came back from far behind to win, withstanding pressure and calmly carding just enough birdies for victory. In the last of the three, he erased a five-stroke deficit with seven straight scores of 3—three pars, three birdies and an eagle—and won on the 38th hole.

In his very first major as a professional, the 1997 Masters, Tiger got off to a brutal start, pushing drives, missing greens and racking up four bogeys for a 40 on the front nine. From the outside it appeared he was nervous and tight, and it was inevitable to wonder, halfway through his first round, if the predictions about his greatness were not, perhaps, out of whack. "I was pretty hot at the way I was playing," Tiger would say afterwards. But he also said "I knew what I was doing wrong." On the practice tee his swing had been fine but now it was loose and wobbly, robbing him of control over his woods and irons. Somehow he needed to alter not only his swing arc but also its tempo, and he needed to do it in a hurry.

The figurative turn from the front nine to the back nine worked like the bell between rounds of a fight. Tiger collected himself, made his adjustments and hit a solid 2-iron off the tee at 10. "I said, all right, here's the deal," Tiger later recalled. "Just make the same swing that you did on this tee shot all the way through the entire back nine ... and from there I hit some good shots and I made everything." On 10, Tiger canned a 10-footer for birdie. Next he sank a 9-iron chip from behind the 11th green for another birdie. He birdied 13 and he eagled 15. A final birdie on 17 gave him a 30 for the back nine, leaving him only three shots out of the lead. When, three days later, Tiger won the Masters by 12 strokes, his 40-30 start became an instant part of his lore.

What it showed, most of all, was his capacity to bounce back from adversity—to turn a potentially disastrous situation into something positive. When the wheels came off, young Tiger could have succumbed to the chaos of the moment, pressing harder to play well and sinking deeper into the mire. Instead, he stayed cool and found a way to turn things around in a very short period of time. He adapted to a changing situation and asserted his control over it. He absorbed all the pressure of the moment—the outsized expectations, the scrutiny of veteran players, the clanking attention of cameramen— and used it as motivation to raise his level of play. Tiger's ability to reroute himself mid-round, depending on what is going wrong with his swing, continually amazes his colleagues. "It's not like there's a big effort to it," says David Feherty. "There are no veins standing out on his forehead. Tiger just becomes more and more centered and more and more calm. To the point where there is no pulse, no blip on the line at all."

This icy resiliency, says performance expert Dr. Jim Loehr, is the mark of a true champion. "It is easy to lead when things are great, but leadership is really demonstrated in these critical moments," says Dr. Loehr. "Does Tiger come apart or look for excuses? No. He thinks, 'This is when I have a chance to do something great. This is when the world needs me more than ever.' What he was doing out there was managing storms, and that is what we do in life. You keep navigating and you become whatever you are capable of becoming, and you don't let the storms be the reason you didn't make it."

In Tiger's case, this is literally true. Many players are unnerved when the weather turns ugly during a round. Whipping winds and sideways rain are just the sort of adverse conditions that a golfer can point to as an excuse for poor play. But not Tiger. "I do like playing in tough conditions," he has said. "It doesn't mean you always play well, but I enjoy that challenge. . . . I don't get bummed out, put it that way."

Tiger's mental fortitude makes such storm management possible, but the specific trait that powers his resolve is the ability to quickly put bad shots behind him. The truth is that Tiger hits his share of lousy shots—surely as many as anyone else on tour. That is the nature of the sport; hitting a golf ball purely each and every time is just about impossible. But from the very beginning Tiger's father taught him to release the negative energy that bad shots produce and not let it carry over into his next shot. Compounding our mistakes—letting the anger and frustration we feel influence what we do *after* we screw up—is a common human failing. Many of us tend to follow one mistake with another. In golf this can be particularly devastating, and so Earl Woods was quick to teach Tiger how to limit the damage. "Inside Tiger there rages a real volcano," says Earl. "He would pound his club into the ground after a bad shot and say, 'I'm sorry daddy, I don't want to do this, it just happens.' And I would say, 'Okay, son, keep working on it.' And gradually he got to the point where his anger did not affect his next shot. He lets it out and immediately forget its, and on the next shot he's all business."

Early in his pro career Tiger occasionally appeared to allow bad shots to affect his mood. His temper and demeanor seemed volatile. He would smash his driver on the tee box like a railroad worker hammering a stake. But that tempestuousness did not last long. "He got rid of all that baggage, all that stuff that followed a bad shot," says Gary McCord. "It was hard to let it go, but nobody expected a 20-year-old kid to come out and be perfect. It was a learning process, and now he just lets the anger go."

Which is not the same as saying he never gets angry. In 2001, Tiger was so frustrated with his play at the Memorial he snapped one of his wedges after dumping a ball in a pond. But, most of the time, Tiger not only controls his anger but also turns it into motivation to follow bad shots with great ones. Late in the final round of the 1999 Memorial he badly flubbed a greenside chip, leaving him an equally difficult 40-foot downhill chip for par. Leading at the time, he was facing a double or even triple bogey that might have sunk his chances to win. Tiger, however, appeared unflustered. He calmly stalked his second chip, calculated the adjustments to his tempo based on his flubbed ball, and played a smooth and delicate swing that showed not a trace of nerves. The ball spun downhill, took its right to left break and dropped, ever so gently, into the cup for par. Given the intensity of the situation, the pressure put on him by his mistake and the degree of difficulty of his next chip, it is easily one of the very best shots Tiger has ever hit. So good that, instead of a triple bogey, fans were treated to a triple fist pump. "What Tiger does with a bad shot is use it as impetus to make him focus even harder," says Bobby Clampett. "Jack Nicklaus also had that. If you wanted to watch Nicklaus at his best, you watched him after he hit a bad shot. That's when he would take it to another level. And that's what Tiger does, too."

It is not surprising, then, that Tiger has always been at or near the top of the PGA's "bounce back" rankings, a statistical category that measures how often a player gets a birdie or better after making a bogey or worse. "I always have an inner peace on the golf course," he has said. "I try and stay calm and never let anything get to me."

This accounts for one of Tiger's most admired accomplishments—from 1999 to 2004 he won 20 out of 24 tournaments that he was leading after two rounds, an astonishing percentage given the numbing pressure second-round leaders inevitably feel on the weekend. During this stretch Tiger converted second-round leads into wins in *18 straight events*. This would not have been possible were Tiger the slightest bit susceptible to big-time pressure. To have maintained his focus, adapted to the chaos and continued to execute time after time after time is, perhaps, the best measure of Tiger's excellence. "He is," the brash golf analyst Johnny Miller once declared, "the greatest frontrunner in the history of the game."

Such is Tiger's poise under pressure that it can have a positive impact even on those victimized by it. At the 2000 AT&T Pebble Beach National Pro-Am, Tiger staged one of golf's most memorable comebacks, making up seven shots in seven holes to defeat Matt Gogel. On his final hole that year, Gogel smashed a wild tee shot that went out of bounds, then compounded that mistake by yanking his approach shot into the Pacific Ocean. But Gogel would turn that indelible defeat into an important lesson. Two years later, he was once again leading at Pebble Beach, and once again he made a huge mistake late in the final round, three-putting the 17th green to fall one shot behind the leader Pat Perez. But then Gogel showed a new composure by scoring a birdie on 18, enough to give him his first

PGA win. "If I learned anything in 2000," he would say, "it was that you have to play all 18 holes."

What Gogel learned was that, under the pressure of adversity, the worst thing we can do is speed up our play or get out of our rhythm or otherwise give in to panic. Champions like Tiger actually slow things down when the heat turns up, taking extra time to think through strategies, focus on technique and assert their control over chaotic situations. There is no reason we cannot do the same in our lives, since even in the midst of absolute chaos there are two things we will always have dominion over—what we think and what we do. "You've got to learn to control your emotions before you control your actions," says Earl Woods. "And that's what Tiger learned from an early age. It's a process."

For a guide along the way to honing our own adaptability, we can do no better than Tiger Woods. It is hard to think of another athlete who has shown more clarity in chaos—who has demonstrated such consistent resolve and immunity to pressure. The guy may be human, but he sure doesn't seem to sweat. In April, 2004, Tiger spent four days training with the U.S. Army at Fort Bragg, North Carolina, where his father once trained. The point of the exercise was to expose him to what his father went through, and to satisfy his appetite for pushing himself to the extreme.

Tiger wore a uniform, took four-mile runs with the 18th Airborne Corps, fired weapons and jumped out of an airplane—not once, but twice. The jumps, from 13,500 feet, sent Tiger plummeting to earth at around 120 mph. On his first landing, Tiger stumbled and fell. The second time, to no one's surprise, he landed on his feet. "I have always said that if I wasn't playing golf for a living, I would be doing something in the military," Tiger said afterwards. "Probably with the Special Forces."

Somewhere, Uncle Sam has his fingers crossed.

PATIENCE:
Ride the Wave

"The way of heaven is like the bending of a bow.
What is high up gets pulled down.
What is low down gets pulled up."

—The Tao Te Ching

"You're going to go through some periods where you're just not at the top of
your game. That doesn't mean that you're going to stay there; that just
means that like anything else, it comes in cycles."

—Tiger Woods

LESSONS COME IN ALL SHAPES AND SIZES—this one was six feet, 200 pounds, and only 12 years old. The hulking boy happened to be paired against Tiger Woods in the first round of the Junior World Championships in San Diego. At the time, Tiger was 11, and built like plywood. Tiger had just jumped age brackets to the 11-12 year-old division—from the 10-and-under category which he had dominated the previous three years. Now, for the first time, he was facing someone significantly bigger and stronger. "So this kid gets up there and drives the first green, and it freaks Tiger out," remembers Earl Woods. "He immediately went into a shell and I wasn't able to communicate with him that whole tournament. He finished way down in the standings and did not win a trophy."

Still, Earl was not done watching his son perform. There was still the awards ceremony to attend. "I wanted to see how he handled himself," says Earl. "And after the ceremony was over, Tiger went up to each of the five kids who won trophies and shook their hands and congratulated them, and they were all laughing and joking, and Tiger was all charm. And that's when I realized: Tiger has learned how to lose."

Look, let's get one thing straight: Tiger Woods hates to lose. Can't stand it, won't abide it, makes him sick. Right there on his list of least favorite things, next to liver and root canals. "Winning is a pleasure for him," says his former coach, John Anselmo. "He always said, 'Second sucks.'" At the same time, Tiger realizes he's going to lose a lot more often than he wins. That is just the nature of the sport he plays—it's unpredictable, unreasonable and unkind. "It's a game of serendipity," says Gary McCord. "Between the spike marks on the greens and the crazy bounces, it's just a very volatile game." Even when Tiger was playing the very best golf of his life—in his magical 2000 season—he lost six of every 10 tournaments he entered. "You look at the greatest champions of all time and their winning percentage in all sports, it's not too good," Tiger remarked in 2003. "We try to put ourselves in a position to win [but] you're not going to win every time."

Which means that even great champions need to learn an important virtue—patience. Even consistent winners must learn to deal with losing all the time. What's more, even elite athletes will inevitably endure periods in which they win infrequently or perhaps not at all. In sports, such slumps can last for weeks and sometimes even years. Thus, how a person handles himself during one of these lulls in fortune can reveal more about him than how he behaves when the going is good. In the case of Tiger Woods, he has demonstrated a profound understanding of the fickle nature of sports—indeed, of life—and has always been humble and gracious during the dips in his play.

More importantly, he has maintained a positive mindset, acting like a champion even when he wasn't one. During the two lengthy downturns in his career—the first when he changed his swing in 1997, and the second when he had knee problems beginning in 2002—Tiger has often appeared frustrated, annoyed with himself and sometimes even a little confused. Yet he has never appeared panicky, hostile, down on himself or impatient. Just as Tiger has shown a great ability to bounce back from bad shots, he knows that stretches of lousy play will inevitably yield to periods of winning golf. As a result, he is able to stay calm and centered even when everyone else is demanding to know what's wrong with him.

In Buddhist thinking, there is a ceaseless interchange between good and bad, heaven and earth, up and down—thus, one can never be in harmony with the universe unless he embraces its cyclical nature. What matters is not the volatility of circumstances; what matters is how we conduct ourselves in such transitory times. "Good people keep on walking whatever happens," the Buddha said. "They do not speak vain words and are the same in good fortune and bad." And, in another passage from the *Dhammapada Atthakatha*, "There are profit and loss, slander and honor, praise and blame, pain and pleasure in this world; the Enlightened One is not controlled by these external things; they will cease as quickly as they come."

What a wonderful thing this is to learn from Tiger Woods: to hold our heads up as high when we are losing as we do when we are winning. Embrace the *whole* experience of being a performer in sports or in life; prove ourselves champions in good times and in bad. The poise and dedication we display during long-term slumps—as opposed to surrendering to frustration and cursing the gods for our misfortunes—will bolster our self-images and hasten our return trip to the top. The worst thing we can do is get down on ourselves when things are bad; we must realize that giving maximum effort and doing everything right is sometimes not enough. We are human, we will fail, and we will fail *a lot*. So where's the sense in flagellating ourselves? "Health permitting, if everything goes right, I may be playing this game as long as Arnold [Palmer] has been," Tiger said in 2001, during a rough stretch with no top-10 finishes in five straight tournaments. "If that's the case, you really can't beat yourself up over every single shot, every single round, every single tournament. You've got to learn from it."

That is not to say it is fine to demand less of ourselves or otherwise slack off during slumps—quite the opposite is true. If all our hard work doesn't seem to make a difference, we must work even harder, not throw up our hands in resignation. We must maintain the standards we set for ourselves regardless of the results our efforts achieve. "They are wise whose thoughts are steady and minds serene, unaffected by good or bad," said the Buddha. Or listen to Tiger struggling to put this mindset into words during a stretch of inferior play in 2001: "I try as hard as I can, and I try to put myself in position, I work very hard at what I do and I love what I do and it's fun for me to go out there and compete, and I'm trying as best as I can and

unfortunately right now it's just not . . . I'm not that far off."
Frustrated? Yes. A little baffled? Sure. Despondent? No way. Slacking
off? Are you nuts? Plenty of others will happily disparage his play and
utter ill pronouncements and try to goad him into blowing his stack.
Meanwhile, Tiger serenely rides out the wave.

Patience—that's the ticket. The calm and uncomplaining
endurance of inevitable events. If you look at a single round of golf
as a metaphor for life, the virtue of patience can be discerned in what
golfers call course management—laying back on risky holes, patiently
accepting pars, then pouncing when the time is right. As a youngster,
Tiger had the reputation of being on full throttle all the time, ignoring risk, challenging every pin, and impatiently attacking at every
opportunity. His high school coach Don Crosby believes that reputation is undeserved. "For a young player, most of the time he had
great course management," says Crosby. "He might have been really
long and wild, but he was very good at managing the course and
knowing where to be and what he needed to do to play from his
favorite distances."

When he turned pro Tiger was once again tagged as a big-hit-
ting, flag-seeking aggressor, and certainly it seemed as if he came out
of his DryJoys every time he took a swing. But very quickly Tiger
reined in his game, sacrificing distance for control and accuracy. Today
he says he swings at roughly 80 percent capacity, and can safely go to
90 percent if he needs a little extra juice. But that still means Tiger is
leaving 10 or 20 yards in his bag. Laying back on certain holes when
you know you have enough firepower to attack requires great
patience—an understanding that, when the time is truly right, your
talents will prevail. This is by no means an easy virtue to achieve.
"Tiger has certainly demonstrated more of an ability to back off
than, say, Greg Norman," says golf historian Sidney Matthew, referring to the swashbuckling Aussie golfer known as the Shark.
"Norman had similar skills, but when it came time to throttle back,
he just couldn't do it. If he had just backed off a few times, he would
have entered another level of greatness."

The patience to pocket your gambler's mentality in favor of a
steadier plan of attack also eluded Tiger's rival Phil Mickelson, who
refused to play it safe in even the most hazardous situations. Yet it was
only after Phil sacrificed some of his awesome length and power for
more shot control—when he finally demonstrated the patience to

trust his own talent and not try to force victory—that he finally won his first major, the 2004 Masters.

Just as Tiger displays patience during the course of a single round, he has calmly weathered both his long-range dry spells. After winning the 1997 Masters, Tiger endured a victory drought, collecting only one trophy in 19 months. In fact the so-called slump was self-induced. Tiger embarked on a complete swing overhaul that he knew would mean far fewer wins on tour. So while he watched his No. 1 ranking slip away and heard predictions about his greatness downgraded, Tiger did not see a reason to panic. Thanks to his Buddha Mind, he understood that great undertakings take great time, and that patience is required to see them through. "Let no one think lightly of good and say to himself, 'Joy will not come to me,'" the Buddha said. "Little by little a person becomes good, as a water pot is filled by drops of water." Or as Tiger patiently explained to reporters pestering him about his poor play in 2004, "I've been making baby steps. Slow and steady progress. When you change things, it doesn't happen overnight." When his swing changes finally came together, Tiger would win 10 of 14 tournaments and seven of 11 majors.

In 2002 Tiger began feeling pain in his left knee. He still won the year's first two majors and finished 2nd at the PGA Championship, but towards the end of the year the pain "was brutal," he would say. "A lot of times, I didn't want to go out there and play. I felt nausea in my stomach because the pain was so great. I had it injected numerous times to play."

Tiger finally had a one-hour surgery on December 12, 2002, to remove benign cysts and fluid from around the anterior cruciate ligament, which had blown his knee up like a balloon. After the surgery he spent a week in bed—"it's driving me crazy," he said—but was soon up and about putting on his rug and chipping into pillows. Still, Tiger realized he had to be patient and allow his knee to heal. He wound up not playing golf for nine weeks, by far his longest stretch away from the game. "I may be rusty," he said on the eve of his return to the tour. "Playing my way into shape is going to take a little time." Tiger made his comeback at the 2003 Buick Invitational, and felt some first-hole jitters. "I remember blocking my first tee shot way right because I didn't trust the knee," he said. "On my next shot, I hit a big 3-wood and didn't even think about my knee. That's when I knew I was all right." The patience he showed in not rushing back from his injury paid off sooner than even Tiger expected: he won the Buick Invitational.

Still, Tiger's play would suffer over the course of the next two years. He didn't win a major in 2003 or 2004, prompting skeptics to reassess predictions that Tiger would easily eclipse Jack Nicklaus's record of 18 major victories. Tiger himself preached the virtue of patience. "I'm still ahead of his pace," he said in 2004. "You know it wasn't going to happen overnight. It's going to take a long time."

As Tiger's troubles continued—sprayed drives, blown leads, mistakes in crucial moments—it became a parlor game to guess why his star had dimmed. Was it his balky left knee? His break-up with swing coach Butch Harmon? His Swedish model girlfriend—and now his wife—Elin Nordegren? All of the above? Tiger wasn't interested in offering excuses. Through it all his mantra remained, "Be patient, it will come."

After struggling at the 2001 Buick Classic, Tiger said, "It's part of the game. You can't play good every week. I tried on every shot and it just really wasn't there." After an unremarkable final round of 70 at the 2001 PGA—the third straight major in which he wasn't really in contention—Tiger told reporters, "It's part of playing sports. You can't play well all the time. You can't have everything go your way, especially in individual sports. It's pretty fickle. There are a lot of things that you need to have happen." And again, after a lackluster third round at the 2003 PGA dropped him to nine over par, Tiger sounded confident his game would soon be back in shape. "I've done it before," he explained. "I did it in '98. Trust me, it won't be the last time. You're going to go through years where you just don't win. But that's okay as long as you keep trying to improve. You have to focus on the positives."

And yet Tiger's return to form was not as imminent as he believed. In 2004, perhaps his toughest year on tour, the frustration he felt at not being able to implement his swing changes was palpable. After a dazzling practice session before the final round of the 2004 PGA—during which he hit several magnificent drives—Tiger badly pulled his tee shot on the 2nd hole. He turned to his caddy Steve Williams and said, almost plaintively, "I didn't hit *one* like that on the driving range."

But even when things were at their worst—when calls to greatness went unanswered and *Sports Illustrated*'s Rick Reilly said Tiger "is basically Kirk Triplett"—Tiger remained inwardly centered and outwardly calm. The occasional club pounded into the turf or epithet muttered too loud? Certainly. Tiger would not be human if he didn't vent his frustration in some way. But in terms of his commitment to his swing changes and overall demeanor on the course, Tiger remained remarkably consistent. "Every one of us has moments where we have doubts and we've got to overcome them," he said in 2004. "That's part of the game. Everybody goes through that." The appropriate response to such moments of doubt? "Just keep playing."

Which bring us to the greatest measure of Tiger's virtuous patience—his two so-called slumps were not really slumps at all. Because Tiger understood he could not win every time—indeed, that he would face stretches where he did not win at all he was able to approach those periods with the same intensity and determination that was evident when he was winning. Whether or not he was taking home trophies was irrelevant to his effort. As the Buddha advised, he remained the same Tiger through both the good and the bad. "There's nobody more majestic," Johnny Miller once observed. "Even when he's struggling, there's something about him."

What is indisputable is that Tiger remained a highly competitive golfer during both of his prolonged dry spells. He frequently contended into the fourth round and did not miss a single cut in some six seasons. "Even when Tiger isn't playing his best, he is still very much in control," says Roger Maltbie. "And that is something that is pretty unique to him." In other words, the effort was the same, the competitive fire was the same, the championship mindset was the same. But because of certain variables—the awkwardness of his swing change, the improved play of his rivals, the vagaries of his sport—the number of wins he posted was not the same.

To Tiger, that mattered less than the consistency of his effort—not because he loved winning any less, but because he understood that losing is part of life. "The whole story of the game of golf is that it's game you cannot master," says Bobby Clampett. "I mean, even Jack Nicklaus won only one out of every 10 tournaments or so. And that's what drew so many people to Tiger: he was dominating a game that has been the hardest in history to dominate. He was doing something nobody really thought was possible."

What Tiger knew, even then, was that along with stretches of transcendent play will come long periods of lesser golf. That, in a nutshell, is life. It is how we handle these downswings—how we ride the wave—that defines as us players and as human beings. "Ordinary people hate nothing more than to be powerless, small and unworthy," says the *Tao Te Ching*. "Yet this is how superior people describe themselves. Gain is loss. Loss is gain."

That would be the *second* lesson Tiger learned that long-ago day when he played against a kid twice his size. "When we got home I said, 'Tiger, what the hell happened on that first hole?'" remembers Earl. "And Tiger said, 'I was scared.' He said, 'Did you see what happened on that hole? He drove the green!'" Earl pointed out that not only did both players par the first hole, but Tiger wound up *winning* the match, even though he would play frightened the rest of the tournament. "I said, 'There's nothing be afraid of, son. Golf is not a game of size or strength.' Tiger thought about it and said, 'Dad, I promise you, I will never be intimidated by another person the rest of my life.' And, to this day, he hasn't."

Be at your best when things are at their worst, and that will make you a winner.

BALANCE:
Gentle Rider

*"Filling to fullness is not as good
as stopping at the right moment.
Oversharpening a blade
causes its edge to be lost."*

—The Tao Te Ching

*"That is really something I look forward to—the times when I can hang out
with any of my friends and relax and do nothing."*

—Tiger Woods

"**Y**OU HAVE TO LOVE EVERYBODY CHASING YOU," Tiger Woods once said of always being pursued. Of course, he was talking about slow-footed golfers, not galloping ten-foot bears. That, he discovered, he didn't love so much.

Tiger was on a fishing trip with pals Mark O'Meara and John Cook, casting for salmon on Kodiak Island off the coast of Alaska. O'Meara, the veteran fisherman in the group, landed a king salmon and dragged it half a mile along the grassy riverbank to their raft. Tiger also caught a nice salmon, and the boys now had enough for a good dinner. That's when Cook yelled, "There's a bear."

Charging along the riverbank: a 10-foot brown bear, following the scent of the salmon and heading straight for the frightened threesome. They all knew a few basics things about brown bears—never make eye contact, for starters, and if it gets too close roll up in a ball on the ground and don't move. But what to do if the bear wants your salmon for dinner, too? As O'Meara and Cook scampered out of the river and towards the raft, Tiger took hold of his big fish as if it was a five-iron. "If they hadn't gotten back in time," he later said, "I would have thrown my fish at the bear." Fortunately the golfers got away. A close call, to be sure, but in the end the bear perfectly served his purpose—it took Tiger's mind off golf. Tiger's adventure on Kodiak Island, while a little more thrilling than originally planned, was all part of his grand design for good living—to be as devoted to his down time as he is to his primary mission. As adept as Tiger is at immersing himself in the game of golf and enlisting every molecule in the fight to win tournaments, he is just as good at dumping his clubs and dropping off the face of the earth. Since turning pro, Tiger has zealously carved out big blocks of free time so he can regularly switch frequencies, indulge a few hobbies and forget about golf altogether. At least two or three times a year the most famous athlete in the country disappears from view and, put simply, ceases being Tiger. "Golf isn't the only thing in his life," says David Feherty. "He has a lot of other interests. Tiger is a well-rounded person, he just doesn't let anyone see him being that."

Tiger's devotion to goofing off is not incidental to his masterful golf, it's a crucial component of it. For Tiger understands a central principle of performance: demanding too much of your mind and body without shutting down the system now and then will likely lead to less progress, not more. Indeed, this is the way of the universe, which yields its treasures only to those who strive for balance in their lives. "If you try to grab hold of the world and do what you want with it, you won't succeed," warns the *Tao Te Ching*. "With Tao, sometimes you move ahead and sometimes you stay back. Sometimes you work hard and sometimes you rest."

Perhaps at this point you're saying to yourself, "Hold on a minute here." We've just spent dozens of pages discussing how Tiger is the most focused, most intense and most dedicated athlete on the planet. And now we're learning he doesn't even pick up a golf club for weeks at a time? Aren't these two things completely contradictory? Not at all. When Tiger is engaged in his mission, he is indeed the hardest-working man in show biz. When the switch is flipped and the clock is ticking, Tiger is *all* business. In the days and weeks before a tournament, Tiger summons his mental focus, marshals his physical strength, and zeroes in on his task with blinding intensity. But Tiger also knows that to enact that game plan he must expend an enormous amount of energy. That level of engagement, he has learned, is not something he can sustain over long stretches of time—it simply puts too much stress on his mind and body. Right after the grueling 2001 Masters, Tiger's fourth major victory in a row, he spent three days in bed with a 104-degree fever. "My body," he admitted, "finally broke down."

For Tiger to be capable of consistently performing at that high level, he must regularly disengage to allow his batteries time to recharge. Finding and defending that time is a priority for Tiger, to whom afternoons on a lazy river are as sacred as a day on the driving range. "If you always have 12 balls in the air, that's quite a feat, but if that's how you operate none of those balls will be extraordinary," says performance expert Dr. Jim Loehr. "When you define for yourself what a successful life is, all the trappings fall off and your realize what things cannot be taken away from you so easily. And then you realize what you have to do to get the energy to make that happen, and you build rituals to support that, and then your life can be extraordinary."

Seeking a balance between work and play is a natural impulse and certainly something we all instinctively try to do. But while many people are casual about their downtime, allowing work issues or other distractions to infringe on its sanctity, some view it as an integral part of the creative process. In *How to Think Like Leonardo da Vinci*, Michael Gelb points out that the great genius liked to alternate "between periods of intense, focused work and rest." The importance of what Gelb calls "incubation" is immeasurable in terms of its impact on performance. "It is well that you should often leave off work and take a little relaxation," da Vinci once wrote, "because when you come back to it you are a better judge." Even ten-minute breaks can help recharge the brain; in Tiger's case—where focusing for days and even weeks at a time is required—much longer breaks come in handy.

Luckily, it seems Tiger has long had a knack for being in balance. When he was just five months old he could stand, perfectly balanced, in the palm of his father's hand. But as his interest in golf turned into a full-blown obsession, it was clear the scales would tip way in favor of his cherished sport. "I love this game to death," Tiger has said. "It's like a drug I have to take." Young Tiger hounded his father to play, entered dozens of tournaments a year and could have set up his own P.O. Box at the local driving range. Save for schoolwork and studying, and the occasional date or party, Tiger's attention to golf was essentially undivided. "I never had to push Tiger and the other golfers; I had to do the opposite and get them to relax and have fun," says Tiger's coach at Stanford University, Wally Goodwin. "They were relentless in what they were trying to achieve. No backing down, no complaining, just going to the range and working on their stuff all the time. Just relentless."

But then, as Tiger got better and better, the very fruit of his excellence—media attention—became an impediment to it. Suddenly there was something else—something insistent, inescapable—that was going to gobble precious moments out of his days. "One time we went to Arizona for a tournament and Tiger had to do this big interview," recalls Goodwin. "Well, our deal as a team was that we went to the course together and then we went to the hotel together. But that particular day it was really cold and there we were waiting for Tiger to finish his interview. Finally the guys went back to the hotel to wait for him there." As early as his teens, Tiger must have realized the demands of his celebrity would set him apart from other golfers and require he come up with his own game plan. Without one, his time would not be his own.

Fortunately, people were watching out for him at home. His exposure to Buddhist teachings surely cued him in to the importance of striking a balance in life. "If energy is applied too strongly it will lead to restlessness," goes a passage in the *Anguttara Nikaya*. "If energy is too lax it will lead to lassitude. Therefore, keep your energy in balance . . . and in this way focus your attention." Tiger's father taught him to listen to his body and heed its demands. To be at your best, Earl Woods advised, sometimes you'll have to put the clubs away. Reluctantly, Tiger did so, though early on he believed himself strong enough to withstand imbalance. "I take time off sometimes because of the mental strain [golf] puts on you," he said in 1997. "But when I'm competing, the will to win overcomes the physical and mental breakdowns."

Even so, Tiger deserved his vacations and he took them. But at the start of his career he could have used a better travel agent. One trip with friends downs to Cancun, Mexico, had to be cut short after mobs of fans seeking photos and autographs swarmed Tiger. Ever since then, he has chosen to vacation further underground—and sometimes under water. One of his newer interests is scuba diving in remote locations. Its appeal is obvious. "The fish," Tiger has said, "don't know who I am." He and his wife Elin have also taken to spearfishing, trolling placid ocean floors for grouper and snapper. Then, of course, there is fly-fishing, taught to him by Mark O'Meara. The two take regular fishing trips to tranquil rivers in far-flung places, including Ireland in the week before British Opens.

The gentle allure of the reel and rod has made the sport one of Tiger's favorite ways to vacuum his brain. "When you are out there, you're just away from a lot of different things and your mind is free to just basically not think about anything," he said by way of explaining his love of fishing in 2001. "Mark and I . . . just kind of kid each other: 'So, have *you* thought about golf?' 'No. You thought about golf?' 'Nope. Thought about any problems?' 'Nope.' It's nice to be able to have that atmosphere . . . to have those kinds of outlets in your life."

Further proof that Tiger is not some hard wired golfbot: he likes playing cards with his buds and catching endless hours of college basketball on TV. He'll tinker with his sports cars and watch the Discovery Channel into the night. He has taken batting practice with his good pal Ken Griffey Jr., and skydived with the Navy Seals. Tiger also spends quality time with his circle of famous friends: Michael Jordan, Charles Barkley and ex-football star Ahmad Rashad. Because they share his competitive drive—and understand his celebrity—they have helped keep him grounded. Quite often, Tiger will speak of perhaps his most preferred pastime—doing nothing. "Didn't touch a club for a while," he said of his long break after the 2001 U.S. Open. "It was nice just kind of not doing much."

To create enough time to properly incubate, Tiger has to stick to a relatively light tournament schedule. While most touring pros play anywhere from 20 to 30 events, Tiger generally signs up for around 18, and would like to cut back on that. "Fifteen tournaments," he once said wistfully. "That would be perfect." He learned his lesson the hard way after playing in 12 events before the June 1997 U.S. Open, leading to the only legitimately missed cut of his pro career later that year. "I played way too much too early for me, and I was fried," he explained of that stretch in 1997. "It's too much of a grind. The whole atmosphere wears you out. Once you get to the tournament site, I have to deal with a lot more than most of the pros."

Since then, Tiger has rarely strayed from the light schedule he lays out early in the year. While PGA officials would surely like to see him in more events, no one can deny his strategy works for him.

Several times Tiger has returned from long layoffs and won his first event, most notably taking the Buick Invitational and two of his next three tournaments after a nine-week break in 2003.

Balance—it is an indispensable facet of Tiger's approach. "It's *all* about balance," he told *Travel & Leisure Golf* in 2002. And yet it has been inevitable to wonder two things about Tiger. Given the intensity of his commitment to golf, isn't he bound to burnout? And, what will happen if he eases up on the gas a little bit? The great amateur golfer Bobby Jones—as dominant in his day as Tiger has been in his—never pretended golf was of paramount importance to him. "My wife and my children came first, then my legal profession," he said. "Finally, and never in a life by itself, came golf." At least early in his career, golf was not just Tiger's top passion, it was his *only* passion. "Tiger is not someone who has been viewed as a renaissance man," says Jones biographer Sidney Matthew. "With Tiger, golf was a life unto itself. But as he matures, we'll see some competing interests. And he may figure, you know, that golf is not the only thing there is."

Tiger has long known how to get away from golf for a while. But in recent years it seems he has also been letting go of the game a little bit. Once all-consuming, the sport is now just a part of Tiger's life. An enormous part, sure, but just a part. He married longtime girlfriend Elin Nordegren in October, 2004, and he has spoken of his desire to start a family. Some Tiger fans may tremble at the notion— what will happen to their dominating hero once he has to run around town picking up Huggies? The truth is, Tiger's commitment to achieving balance in his life—to not going too hard at any one endeavor for too long—should not waver no matter how his life changes. In golf terms, that means Tiger will never be anything less than a ferocious competitor. "Because I've become more rounded in my life, it's made it easier to play golf," he recently told David Feherty. "I know that I used to get so consumed by it and had sleepless nights . . . and because I've had a great relationship with Elin, because I got interested in diving a little bit more, because I've traveled the world a little bit more, my life is so much better now than it ever has been. And hopefully that will translate into more wins."

And so Tiger continues to strive for the perfect balance in his life, aware, as we all should be, that our time on earth is too short to shut our eyes to any of its beauties. "Thus shall ye think of all this fleeting world," the *Diamond Sutra* tells us. "A star at dawn, a bubble in a stream; a flash of lightning in a summer cloud; a flickering lamp, a phantom, and a dream." The only way to truly appreciate the vast wonder of existence—and to truly honor the gifts that each of us have been given—is to loosen our grip on one thing, so that we may touch another. "The soft overcomes the hard in the world," says the *Tao Te Ching*, "as a gentle rider controls a galloping horse."

Or even, in some cases, a galloping bear.

EXUBERANCE:
Share Your Heart

"The sage doesn't hoard. He increases his treasure
by working for his fellow human beings. He increases
his abundance by giving himself to them."
    — *The Tao Te Ching*

"I care a lot about golf, and I care about kids. I'm going to share whatever I
can with them. I'll share them my heart. That's about all I can offer."
    — *Tiger Woods*

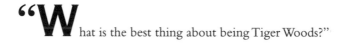

"**W**hat is the best thing about being Tiger Woods?"

That's the question Jacob Washington, a junior golfer from Allentown, Pennsylvania, lobbed at Tiger during the Q&A portion of a youth golf clinic in Anaheim, California. Held on a steamy day in August, 2004, the event brought Jacob and hundreds of other children to the vast bleachers assembled on the driving range of the H.G. "Dad" Miller Golf Course, the 6,025-yard municipal layout where Tiger played his high school golf not all that long ago. Dad Miller, the kind of flat, largely featureless course where you have to cross a street to get from the ninth to the tenth holes, would soon undergo an astonishing transformation thanks to its most famous fan, but we'll get to that part of the story in a minute. On that sizzling summer day, Jacob and the other kids were there to see Tiger put on a show— and to ask a few personal questions.

So what *is* the best thing about being Tiger Woods?

The man himself, wearing a wireless mike and twirling an iron as he stood before the crowd, did not hesitate. "I have to say probably a few things are pretty cool," he said. "One is I get a chance to do what I absolutely love to do, which is compete and play golf. Number two, it is pretty nice, on Friday and Saturday nights when restaurants are busy, I can call up and get a table."

Everyone laughed at the restaurant crack, but the first part of Tiger's answer came straight from his heart. For it is this, among his many virtues, that makes them all possible: Tiger Woods is crazy about his job. He had the good fortune of finding his calling early, and since then his passion for it has seemed limitless. When we watch him play—when we take note of his fullness of approach and expansiveness of spirit—it seems we are watching a man's genuine joy at being alive. We understand right away that what we are seeing is *authentic*— that this is someone doing what he should be doing, and doing it properly. There is nothing phony or adulterated about his quest, no artifice to his artistry, and that purity of purpose gives us a great big window into his heart.

That, above all else, is the wonder of Tiger Woods: he allows us the vicarious thrill of connecting vividly with his world and, through it, our own. "He's making millions of dollars but he looks like a kid out there," says David Feherty. "He has a kind a naiveté that you see in you children's faces when they don't want to come in from the sandbox because they're having too much fun. Most of us grow out of it or become self-conscious, but there's a lack of self-consciousness in Tiger that I've not seen in any other athlete. It's a kind of simple exuberance, and it's a beautiful thing to see."

It is also, in this difficult world, something quite rare. Think how exceedingly easy it can be to take our lives for granted, to lose our capacity for joy in an endless cycle of chores. Those not fully committed to their lives plod along under a pretense of fulfillment. The face they present to the world is grimaced, perhaps even glum.

Think for a moment—what face do you present to the world? Can you say that what you devote your life to gives you the vitality you crave? Can you look at what you produce and say there is blood running through it? Are you, as the great scholar Joseph Campbell advised, following your bliss? "If you do follow your bliss, you put yourself on a kind of track that has been there all the while, waiting for you," he said in *The Power of Myth*, "and the life you ought to be living is the one you *are* living."

This is quite obviously the case with Tiger. The best actor in the world could not fake the enthusiasm he shows for golf. "Certainly I think that exuberance is genuine," says Sidney Matthew. "I think that his mother and his father loved him very much, and I don't think that someone like Ben Hogan got that message. And you can really tell the difference. It shows."

Take, for instance, the most iconic manifestation of Tiger's exuberance: his flame-throwing, full-bodied fist pump. Employed after especially masterful or decisive shots, it is a cathartic marvel of kinetic energy—the right hand packed tightly into a fist; the right arm puncturing the sky with a violent, slashing uppercut; the body rocked backwards by the force of the punch and the right leg kicking slightly forward for balance; the face, finally, contorted by a fierce primal roar. Repeat twice and you have Tiger's resplendent fist-pump dance, which can whip already frenzied crowds to fever pitches and may be the most electrifying expression of pleasure in sports.

Not that Tiger was the first golfer to pump his fist after a good shot. Historians generally credit Arnold Palmer with introducing emotion to golf, exhilarating crowds with his skyward visor toss and shattering the institutional stoicism of muted geniuses like Ben Hogan and Bobby Jones. Others firebrands followed: the garrulous Lee Trevino, who didn't pump his fist so much as deliver a smashing right cross; the boisterous Spaniard Seve Ballesteros, whose flair for the theatrical produced a dramatic pump; the emotional Payne Stewart, king of the lights-out, heart-on-his-sleeve lunge.

But it was Tiger who took the fist pump to a new level. When he was only six years old "he started doing this thing where he raised his arms when he holed a putt," remembers his then-coach Rudy Duran. "It was a little less intense than what he would do later on, but when Tiger did something good, you could tell. He definitely felt the thrill of victory. He was very excited about his good shots."

Still, Tiger waited for the perfect moment to formally unveil the fist pump: the denouement of the 1994 U.S. Amateur on the TPC at Sawgrass in Jacksonville, Florida. After holing a critical putt from the fringe on the 17th hole—the course's fabled island green—Tiger erupted into a volcanic victory dance, scurrying across the green while slamming an imaginary foe with uppercuts. "That was the first time I saw him do it, and it was the most emotion I've ever seen him show," says John Anselmo, Tiger's swing coach at the time. "And from then on, that arm kept flying. With me, he had always been kind of reserved, so I don't know where that came from." Tiger's outbursts became his trademark, the signature on his masterpieces, and their intensity introduced a new physicality to golf. To the point where, as *Travel & Leisure Golf* declared, "Woods transformed the motion into the most identifiable symbol of the game since the golfer silhouette first appeared on the PGA Tour logo in 1970."

Yet as he matured, Tiger grew less demonstrative, mothballing the turbo pump in favor of a more sedate fist waggle. He explained that his spasms of excitement expended too much energy, leaving him susceptible to lulls in his play. "Learning how to control my emotions," he said, "has been a part of the natural evolution of learning how I can play better." But fewer fist pumps does not mean diminished joy. There are other ways to tell that Tiger is having a blast out there. We have spoken of his intensity, his unbreakable focus, his aloneness. Indeed, for most of a round, Tiger appears utterly joyless. "He's not out there on a laugh mission," says Roger Maltbie. "This is not jolly golf. What Tiger is doing is very important to him, and the spectators and viewers can see the sense of urgency he has."

Now and then, however, usually once or twice a round, the cocoon cracks. What we then get to see is Tiger's smile, a phenomenon unto itself. The surprise of seeing his granite mask of concentration crumble—sort of like seeing Abe Lincoln suddenly wink on Mount Rushmore—makes the smile a wonderfully embracing gesture, the tip-off that Tiger is, after all, human, just like us. "I think the whole crowd is out there waiting for Tiger to smile," says Jim Huber. "They want to see him happy, see him twirl his club and shake his head and grin like a kid. I certainly wait for Tiger to smile, because it's such a magical moment. It's so real, there's nothing put on about it. It doesn't happen too often, but when it does he lights up the whole golf course." Tiger's smile "is the most important weapon he has," says David Feherty. "It's electric. It makes the hair on the back of your arms stand up. Tiger makes you think, 'God, it must be amazing to feel like that.' And when he smiles his look tells you, 'Yeah, it is.'

Through the simple act of smiling, Tiger illustrates the essence of Buddhist thinking: retain your childlike heart. Never lose the sense of awe and wonder you had as a child, nor the inherent compassion you felt for those around you. Strip away the cynicism and expectations built up by years of disappointments and approach the world with the openness of someone seeing it for the first time. Allow the wonder of existence to course through your being. "Those who enjoy life," says the *Tao Te Ching*, "are wiser than those who employ life."

To achieve such a state of exuberance requires an honest appraisal of our goals, lest we spend our lives hurriedly chasing all the wrong dreams. "The deluded, imagining trivial things to be vital to life, follow their vain fancies and never attain the highest knowledge," says *The Dhammapada*. "But the wise, knowing what is trivial and what is vital, set their thoughts on the supreme goal and attain the highest knowledge."

Put another way, focusing exclusively on our narrow self-interests reflects a closed mind and a closed heart. How, then, can we open our minds and hearts? The Dalai Lama says we must cultivate something called loving-kindness, which he defines as the wish that every human being be happy. It is not enough to wish happiness for ourselves and for our loved ones; we must wish it—and seek it—for the entire world. This may sound like some fuzzy fortune-cookie wisdom, but it is actually a very practical directive. To cultivate loving-kindness "it is important to start by taking a specific individual as a focus of our meditation, and we then extend the scope of our concern further and further, to eventually encompass and embrace all sentient beings," the Dalai Lama said in a speech in New York City in 1999. "We work on one person at a time."

Earl Woods had another name for loving-kindness: he called it caring and sharing. "To care and share is the family motto," says Earl. "Tiger has said it is the most important lesson he learned, to give of himself." Earl also taught his son that by focusing on one person at a time, Tiger could very well change the world.

And that is just what Tiger has audaciously set out to do. In 1996, he and his father started the Tiger Woods Foundation, which today is the main arm of Tiger's vast charity machine. Most modern athletes are affiliated with charitable groups and devote large blocks of time to helping people in their communities and across the nation. Many have started their own foundations, just like Tiger. What is so exceptional about Tiger's Foundation is that he started it at the same time he turned pro. It has always been an integral, and not incidental, part of who he is and what he is trying to accomplish—every bit as important to him, Tiger has said, as his golf game. "He knew right away that he was going to be someone that potentially everyone watched and listened to," says Gary McCord. "He was determined to give something back to the game before he even started playing it."

In its short history the Foundation has awarded hundreds of grants to youth-oriented programs in dozens of cities and directly helped more than one million children discover and achieve their goals through its Start Something initiative. It has also raised millions of dollars through a variety of events and tournaments, including the annual Tiger Jam, a benefit concert held in Las Vegas (Prince was the headliner in 2004), and the Target World Challenge, a 72-hole event open to only 16 elite players and hosted by Tiger himself.

Despite the current scope of the Foundation—already one of the largest charitable organizations presided over by an athlete—it turns out Tiger and his father have only just begun. The year 2005 will see the opening of the Tiger Woods Learning Center, quite possibly the most ambitious undertaking ever by a jock. Created with $5 million in seed money from Tiger—or just about everything he won playing golf in 2001—and huge gobs of cash from corporate sponsors, the $25 million Center is a 35,000-square foot educational haven with seven classrooms, a computer lab, a multimedia center and a spacious student lounge.

The Center is situated in one of the bleaker sections of Anaheim, California, on the 14 acres that used to be the driving range at Tiger's beloved Dad Miller golf course, which itself will receive a generous face lift as part of the project. Its goal is to offer thousands of children from ages 8 to 17 a place to hang out in the hours after they finish with their regular schooling; the premise is that these are pivotal hours for inner city children precisely because of the absence of constructive places to go. No one will teach these kids how to hit a flop shot or knock down a five iron. Instead they'll be tutored in math, science and the language arts. The emphasis, as it is in all of Tiger's forays into helping children, will be on giving them the skills to achieve their individual dreams.

Now here comes the truly ambitious part: if it works in Anaheim, Team Woods wants to take the concept nationwide. "Our mission is to empower young people to reach their highest potential by initiating and supporting community-based programs *for all of America's children*," Earl Woods declared at a press conference at Dad Miller to raise awareness about the Center. "That is not an idle statement. It was carefully thought out by Tiger and myself . . . we are committed to America's children." So this is what they mean by all that "change the world" stuff. "Golf has been good to me, but the lessons I've learned transcend the game," Tiger has said about his Foundation. "I'm now trying to pass these invaluable lessons on and show kids how they can be applied to every aspect of life."

And, as the Dalai Lama advised, he's doing it more or less one kid at a time. One of the more direct ways Tiger reaches out to children is through the four or five golf clinics he holds each year. So far, Tiger has hosted 34 such clinics—mostly for inner-city children from across the country. At the sweltering August 2004 clinic in Anaheim—just a few three-woods away from Disneyland, home to other larger-than-life characters with animal names—junior golfers from Pennsylvania, Illinois, North Carolina and Jamaica enjoyed private lessons from Tiger as well as his customary exhibition of skills. To start things off, sixteen youngsters in traditional Thai costumes performed historical dances under the watchful eye of Tiger's mother, Tida, sitting in the front row of the bleachers (afterwards, Tida brought each child a cup of water). Next, several Navy "leapfrogs"— members of its crack parachute team—jumped out of a Coast Guard C-130 flying 6,000 feet above the golf course. Trailing green and pink smoke, they landed one after another within a few feet of a target on the driving tees. The children were told Tiger had twice jumped from a plane with Navy Seals, and also learned that parachutists plummet to earth at speeds around 120 mph—ironically, the approximate speed of Tiger's ferocious swing.

After a speech about trust and respect from Earl Woods—which some children would later say affected them more than anything Tiger said—the man of the hour carted in from the back of the range to strains of "Eye of the Tiger." With his very first swing, he plunked a five-foot green sign 100 yards out, just as he said he would ("Not bad, huh?"). Tiger followed that with sweeping fades and honking draws—shots that flew over one zip code and wound up in another. He unleashed his patented 2-iron stinger and pounded the 15-degree loft three-wood he has played with since 1998. He took full swings that sent the ball 10 feet, and half swings that launched it more than 200 yards. When he calmly strode to his bag and slid the tiger head cover off his driver, the crowd collectively tittered. His blasts to the back of the range were practically seismic, but Tiger emphasized that during his swing, "I was in perfect balance." Tiger finished with his signature flourish—bouncing a ball off the blade of his club, this time even doing it with a driver.

It was a thoroughly polished piece of showmanship with a craftily hidden agenda. Ostensibly the exhibition was a golf tutorial, but the subtext to Tiger's trickery was that anything is possible—or at least a lot more than many children are nurtured to believe. That is also the goal of Tiger's more intimate lessons with some of the lucky invitees. At Dad Miller, seven youngsters were give some private time with Tiger, who watched them swing and provided a tip or two. "He said my posture was messed up and he told me to straighten up," says 15-year-old Angel Gonzalez, who came into the clinic with only three years golf experience and came out with the ambition of one day turning pro. Corrine Kahn was nervous when Tiger made his way to her, but still managed to hit four nifty seven-irons with him watching. "He said I was a fast learner and had a good swing," says Corrine, who had her picture taken with Tiger and pasted it on her school binder. She, too, hopes to make it to the tour one day.

These are dreams youngsters like Angela and Corrine would have had a hard time harboring even 10 or 15 years ago. But whether they make it or not doesn't matter. In this case it is the size of the dream that counts. Tiger is giving children not normally exposed to opportunities a reason to believe they can be anything they want. If they don't grow up to be great golfers, perhaps they will be great surgeons or great lawyers or great classical musicians. For sure they will have a better shot of becoming great somethings, simply because a superstar like Tiger thinks they can. "We all went to Disneyland afterwards and it was great, but the real magic was Tiger Woods," says Corrine's mother, Noreen. "He is giving so much back to these kids and pulling them off the streets and giving them a focus. I mean, meeting Tiger will stay with Corrine for the rest of her life. It was the chance of a lifetime just to see him and to realize, `Hey, if I work a little harder, this is what can happen to me.'"

What makes Tiger such a gifted emissary, what allows him to really get through to children, is that he is, by all accounts, the real deal. "You cannot fool a kid," says Earl. "If you are genuinely inter-ested in a child, they know it and respect it. If you are not, they know that, too." Earl recalls one clinic Tiger hosted in New York City. The invited children were "stone-cold inner city kids," says Earl. "Hard to the core." Tiger came out, took the microphone and said—nothing. "He just stood there, didn't say a word," remembers Earl. "This went on for the longest time. And you could hear all the kids get quiet. And it just got more and more quiet. And finally Tiger said—and I never heard him say this before or since— 'Today, I am going to speak to you from my heart. I didn't choose to be a role model, you chose me. And I will tell you that I will do the best that I can to be a positive role model for you. But you, too, can be role models. And I want you all to strive to be role models for someone else.'"

And so it becomes clearer and clearer: Tiger Woods intends to change the world, one bright-eyed kid at a time. If each child he influences can touch someone else, and then that someone gets through to another someone...well, you do the math. "This is what I really want to leave behind when I'm done," Tiger said of his Foundation in 2001. "When I'm through breathing I would like to see this organization global."

Yet Tiger's message, though aimed at children, hardly applies only to them, for the desire to reach one's potential knows no demo-graphic bounds. Tiger seems as capable of inspiring adults as he is of impressing their kids. Indeed, some have speculated that Tiger will seek an even broader forum and, sooner rather than later, run for political office. Senator Woods? Governor Woods? Well, would you want to be the one to run against him?

Of course, this assumes that he will one day tire of golf, and that is another subject of speculation. "People always ask me, 'Will Tiger burn out?'" says his college coach, Wally Goodwin. "He might, but I'm not even close to thinking that is possible. Because Tiger is really out there playing for the kids, and my gut feeling is that motivation will last a lot longer than if he were just doing it for himself. A huge part of Tiger is helping kids."

Let us hope, at least for now, that Goodwin is right. For the kind of exuberance Tiger displays—both on the golf course and in the company of children—is a rare and truly thrilling thing. It should, like all of his virtues, move us to question our own commitment to what we do. Are we trying to cultivate loving-kindness in our lives?

Have we decided to share our hearts with the world? How is it that our friends, our loved ones, our children, can tell that we feel joyous to be alive? In what ways does our exuberance manifest itself? What is our fist-pump?

Or, to paraphrase young Jacob Washington from Allentown, Pennsylvania, "What is the best part about being *you?*"

PART FOUR:

THE TIGER
IN US ALL

What do you call plummeting 13 stories in a runaway elevator at faster than the speed of gravity? The folks at California's Disneyland call it a thrill ride. But to the handful of kids inside the Twilight Zone Tower of Terror, it would have been more accurate to call it an "I'm-so-scared-I-can't-breathe" ride. Eleven-year-old Corrine Kahn felt a whole swarm of butterflies in her stomach as the rickety service elevator climbed 183 feet in the air. She knew that a few moments later, with its doors wide open, the elevator would plunge to earth. About the only reassuring thing was that the world's most famous athlete was on the elevator with her. "When he first came on the ride and everyone was around him, I said to him, 'I'm nervous,'" recalls Corrine, one of several kids invited to attend a youth golf clinic in Anaheim, California, and to ride the Tower of Terror with their host. "And he said, 'What's there to be nervous about? There's no bogeyman here.'" While everyone else screamed their lungs out "Tiger was pretty calm," says Corrine. "During the ride he wasn't screaming or anything."

You couldn't ask for a better seat mate on a freefalling elevator than a guy with ice water in his veins. Of course, we're not all lucky enough to have Tiger Woods with us in pressure situations, and so it seems we must face our fears alone.

But here's the thing: we *can* turn to Tiger for assurance when things get hairy; we *can* enlist Tiger as a tour guide through the dark and the dire. For we have, in the example of his speech and conduct, a template for how to handle ourselves in just about any situation. That, in a nutshell, is the message of this book: that as we embark on our own adventures, no matter what they are, we have the lessons of one who preceded us on the path to excellence. "Even the gods emulate those who are awakened," says the *Dhammapada*. "One like the Buddha is hard to find; such a one is not born everywhere."

Such a one we have, living and breathing, amongst us here and now. If you have made it this far in our journey through Tiger's virtues, then perhaps you agree with me that he is, in mythological terms, a heroic figure—someone whose deeds and demeanor make him eminently worth emulating. Certainly that is where my interest in Tiger has taken me.

But please don't think I am deifying Tiger—that would be a silly thing to do. What kind of deity loves Mortal Kombat and was nicknamed "Urkel" in college? Let us never allow his brilliance to obscure Tiger's humanity—he is flawed, stubborn, goofy, vulnerable, as susceptible to failure and open to heartbreak as any of us. When he was six he had a speech impediment and took special reading classes for two years; to this day the impediment makes it hard for him to speak foreign languages. He's got nasty allergies and has had to gobble Claritins like breath mints. He's known as a notoriously bad tipper—definitely a deity no-no. And he has had to overcome adversity from an early age. On his first day of kindergarten some boys tied him to a tree and taunted him with racial slurs. He would later have nightmares about being targeted and killed by an assassin. As he grew up he was not permitted to play certain golf courses because of his race, and so could never forget he was a black athlete in a white sport. All of which makes his triumph that much more remarkable. "If Tiger was going to make it, he had to work harder than everyone else," says golf historian Sidney Matthew. "To be admired like Tiger is, there usually has to be some perception of overcoming adversity. Bobby Jones had an intestinal disease as a kid and almost died. Ben Hogan had to endure the suicide of his father. With Tiger, his father taught him he would have to overcome society's discriminations. And so we fundamentally acknowledge that this quest was necessary for Tiger to overcome all that."

Tiger's hero-quest would not be complete, however, if he did not share his discoveries with us. And, indeed, he has sprinkled the clues we need to get through our own adventures in his performances on the golf course. It is like the Greek myth of Ariadne's thread. The daughter of King Minos, Ariadne vowed to help the man she loved, the dashing Theseus, find a way out of a labyrinth and avoid the dreaded Minotaur if he agreed to marry her. Wisely, she sought the help of Daedalus, who had constructed the maze. He gave her a simple skein of thread, which Theseus could affix to the entrance and unwind as he passed through the labyrinth. With it, he had a way out; without it, he would be lost.

In the same way, we can pick up the clues Tiger has given us and more easily navigate the labyrinth of our lives. "We have only to follow the thread of the hero-path," Joseph Campbell says in *The Hero With a Thousand Faces*. "Where we had thought to travel outward, we shall come to the center of our own existence; where we had thought to be alone, we shall be with all the world." In ancient times monsters like the Minotaur represented society's vast unknowns—its dark forests, the far reaches of the earth, the unintelligible forces of nature and the destructive power of human sickness. But now that technology has opened the whole world to us, the only demons that remain are those that reside inside us. The only darkness we must face is the darkness of fear and doubt. Thus, as Campbell tells us, "the modern hero-deed must be that of questing to bring to light again the lost Atlantis of the coordinated soul."

That's where Tiger comes in. Remember when he told his father "I am at peace"? And all the times he has spoken of "being in balance"? That is what Campbell means by the coordinated soul. And it is what the Buddha meant by conquering ourselves before we can conquer anyone or anything. The things that Tiger has done to overcome fear and doubt can, if we allow them, serve as clues to help us as we prepare for our own adventures. The secrets of the universe are right there in the golf of Tiger Woods.

And yet Tiger's wisdom won't mean anything to us unless we marry it to actual experience. His virtues are not the lessons themselves but rather the inspiration; we can only truly learn by doing things for ourselves.

When Tiger was young, he loved nothing more than practicing at the driving range. His high school coach Don Crosby remembers that the boys on his team—who much preferred playing to practicing—had to pass the driving range on their way to the first tee, and would always see Tiger there, methodically pounding shot after shot. Tiger wasn't even in high school yet, but already his practice habits put his future teammates to shame. "Well one day I came out and saw all the guys at the practice range and not just hanging around the first tee," says Crosby. "Little by little they had noticed what Tiger was doing, and how good he was." Tiger's example got the boys to the driving range, but it was their own hard work that helped them improve. "Tiger isn't teaching anything, he's just being himself," says Earl Woods. "But that's not to say you can't learn from him. It's all there for people. All they have to do is absorb it."

Tom Kahn, whose daughter Corrine attended the Anaheim golf clinic in August 2004 and rode the Tower of Terror with Tiger, remembers his brief meeting with Tiger when he picked up Corrine after the ride. "I just wanted to thank him for everything, because he paid for us to go to California and stay in a nice hotel, and he gave her a private lesson and went on the ride with her and all these wonderful things," he says. "And so when he walked by I said, 'Tiger, thank you for everything.' And he didn't say, 'You're welcome,' he said, 'Thank you.' It was just a little thing but I thought it was interesting. And so now I've started doing that with other people. When they thank me, I thank them back. It feels like a nice thing to do. And Tiger kind of influenced me on that."

Watch, listen, put into practice—sometimes it is as easy as that. Perhaps it is just a little thing, but as Lao Tzu advised, we must "cross the universe one step at a time." This, then, is the simple way we can begin to unleash the Tiger in us all. Look—certainly it would help at this point if I were some sort of life counselor, or motivational expert, or doctor of psychology, and not just a sportswriter. Sadly, I cannot offer any Steps for Self-Mastery or Game Plan for Getting What You Want. Not qualified, not interested. But I can talk about what I think are the most important clues available to us in Tiger's virtuousness—let's call them five adjustments we can make to the way we think and act. It is not about trying to mimic everything Tiger does or running down his list of virtues and checking them off one by one. Each of our lives is different—different demands, different obligations, different destinations—and so not everything that works for Tiger may work for all of us. Even Tiger cannot have everything in sync all the time. What matters is that we set ourselves on the right path, because if we do even small adjustments can produce exponentially satisfying results. "All the life-potentialities that we never managed to bring to adult realization . . . are there, for such golden seeds do not die," said the brilliant scholar Joseph Cambell. "If only a portion of that lost totality could be dredged up into the light of day, we should experience a marvelous expansion of our powers, a vivid renewal of life."

So let's start dredging, and let's do it by adhering to this simple premise—it is good and wise to take role models. If your goal is to become a professional golfer, it is hard to find a better role model than Tiger Woods. "I am a student of this game and of the golf swing, and what Tiger does fits all the criteria for excellence," says Gary McCord. "He is pretty much off the charts on all fronts. I get extreme joy just watching him play this game."

But if golf is not your bag, find someone who is at the very pinnacle of your chosen field. And don't just stop at one role model, take several—that's what Tiger did. "When I was young, I looked up to a lot of players for a lot of different reasons," he has said. There was Nicklaus for his drive, Ben Hogan for his driving, Ben Crenshaw for his putting, and so on. Tiger studied them all and seized on what he felt he could use in his game. We must similarly take advantage of the examples others have set for us, not by merely copying what they did but by using what they learned to chart our own path to excellence. Tiger, in particular, serves up a lot of clues we can use—he has unspooled quite a length of hero-thread. But whomever we choose as a role model—if we choose wisely—will surely provide us with a wealth of hard-earned lessons and insight. Allow their inspirational examples to get you to the driving range, and then you can take over from there.

Which brings us to our next mental adjustment—to keep ourselves on a good path we must build rituals. Going to the driving range because Tiger does is wonderful. But you can't just do it once or twice, you have to do it all the time, or at least every Tuesday, Thursday and Saturday. Rituals, as performance expert Dr. Jim Loehr pointed out, are the way we insure we will have the energy we need to achieve our goals. They are the sacred time during which we can do the essential work of bettering ourselves. Of course, we cannot always carve huge blocks of time out of our packed schedules to devote to, say, practicing the violin, if our dream is to play at Carnegie Hall. But we must understand that, if this is our dream, we cannot accomplish it without some sacrifice. It will require exceptional devotion and impose seemingly impossible demands. The key, then, is to keep at it—to keep to our rituals. Be consistent in setting aside time to do your work, even if you can't always set aside as much time as you like. Do not neglect to do your duty, as the Buddha advised. But also remember that not even Tiger burns his candle to the nub every time out. "Some days I practice 15 hours, some days 15 minutes," he has said. "Some days it's just not there." Even so, he added, "there are a lot more 15 hour days than 15 minute days."

Of course, Tiger is one of the most disciplined athletes ever to break a sweat. But discipline, like all his virtues, is just a state of mind. We can become disciplined simply by believing that we are disciplined. If you create rituals and stick to them, you will be exhibiting good discipline without even thinking about it. Soon it will be an integral part of who you are, and you will be thought of as a disciplined person. "We become," said the Buddha, "what we think." So think about what it will take to achieve your goal—based on the examples of those who went before you—and build the rituals you need to do that sacred work. "Don't think you can attain total awareness and whole enlightenment without proper discipline and practice; this is egomania," said Lao Tzu. "Appropriate rituals channel your emotions and life energy toward the light."

Okay, so now you've got a role model and you've got a ritual—what next? What Tiger has taught us is that the way to get the most out of your labor—the way to maximize your abilities—is to always be present when you work. Put this one in the easier-said-than-done category. What does it mean to be present? Isn't that what we are doing when we sequester ourselves to hit six-irons or play the violin? What more can we do besides show up and get down to business? Aren't we present just by being present? Well—no. Being present requires a mental adjustment, and a tricky one at that. Think about all the times you've done something but not really done it— the times you've absently played a video game or half-cleaned your room or talked to a friend while thinking about something else or even watched a movie without really watching it. Who among us hasn't spaced out from time to time?

Well, being present is the opposite of spacing out. It means devoting ourselves totally to the task at hand. Not 95 percent or 99 percent, but 100 percent. Complete and absolute immersion in what we are doing is the way we get the most out of our skills—the only way we can reach our full potential. When we draw the bow across the string we cannot think about what we'll wear to Carnegie Hall. We must see nothing but the bow and the string and hear nothing but their heavenly sound. The problem is our mind is capable of storing so much information it is extremely difficult to keep it pinned on just one thing. The mind wants to wander, and sometimes it is good that it does, but we cannot allow it to wander when we are doing our good work. "The mind is desperate to fix the river in place," said Lao Tzu. "Possessed by ideas of the past, preoccupied with images of the future, it overlooks the plain truth of the moment."

So here it is, as best as I can figure it: in your quest to be the best at something, your mind is the enemy. It must be conquered, pinned down, wrestled into place and afforded no quarter. Lose this battle and you've lost the war. So think of your mind as an adversary who is much weaker than you—it can be trained and it can be contained, and you're just the one to do it. Impose your will over your mind, and you will discover what it means to be present.

Now comes another absolutely essential mental adjustment—try your best to live creatively. Yes, heed your role models, but choose your own path and dazzle everyone with your originality. Don't just live—play the game of life. Engage with the world in a way few people consistently do; embrace life's ambiguities and contradictions and appreciate the fullness of its experience. This is Tiger bouncing the ball on the face of his club—he's not only striving to achieve self-mastery, he's having a blast doing it. Leonardo da Vinci spoke of saper vedere, or knowing how to see. As Michael Gelb notes in *How to Think Like Leonardo da Vinci*, the great artist once lamented that the average human "looks without seeing, listens without hearing, touches without feeling, eats without tasting, moves without physical awareness, inhales without awareness of odor or fragrance, and talks without thinking."

Yikes, do we really do all that? If you suspect that you might, then you are not living creatively. To do so, we must have a lusty curiosity about the world around us—an appetite for knowledge and experience. Sure, Tiger seems pretty focused on that little dimpled ball. But did you know he also knows the Latin names for all the trees he passes on fairways? The good news is that we all possess the tools we need to engage with the world is such a vivid way; it is a matter of summoning them from their dark and musty shed. When you are interested in something, follow that interest as far as takes you. Go ahead and take it to the extreme. Activate your curiosity and really discover something instead of just settling for a blurry snapshot. And in this way you trigger your own creativity. In life there are creators and spectators—idols and the idle. Which do you wish to be?

"If you bring forth what is inside you, what you bring forth will save you," says the Gospel of Thomas. "If you don't bring forth what is inside you, what you don't bring forth will destroy you."

Now that you've come this far you might as well go all the way, and that means you must open your heart. In Buddhist imagery the mind is often pictured in the middle of the chest, right where the heart should be. To open the heart is to open the mind, and both of these are deliberate decisions we must choose to make. In Greek mythology a hero must be ready for the experience that awaits him; if he is distracted or unprepared to absorb its lessons, he is ineligible to travel the hero-path. In the same way we must be ready for our adventure. We must—knees bent, arms out, poised in a crouch—be prepared to handle whatever the world throws our way. This readiness, or openness, can be the difference between making progress and spinning our wheels. "Everybody starts out an ordinary human being," says Dr. Jim Loehr. "Tiger may have special gifts, but we all have gifts. The question is, how do we get from being ordinary to being truly extraordinary? That is what we must figure out."

Loehr's concept of "full engagement" as the key to being extraordinary is not at all dissimilar to the idea of opening our hearts. Nor is Joseph Campbell's idea of saying yes to our adventure. We must welcome, rather than resist, the impositions of our world, for it is through interaction and experience that we gain true wisdom. Make sure the face you present to others is neither grimaced nor glum, but radiant, reflecting your joy at being alive and inviting others to feel it, too. Something as simple as changing your expression can make an enormous difference in how others perceive and approach you.

To open your heart is to create a two-way channel, allowing the goodness of people in and letting your own unique gifts benefit the world. Thus we must make this most important of all mental adjustments—vow to seek the truth of who you are, not hide behind barriers erected to keep others out. And the only way to get at this truth is to open our hearts and minds. "That is the cement that holds the whole thing together," says Earl Woods. "You have to come from truth in order to really improve yourself. The system won't work if you are not being truthful. It all starts with how you see yourself."

This is the essence of the message imparted by the golf of Tiger Woods. His life evokes his better character, and ours can, too; he is achieving his true potential, and so can we. Heroes inspire the possibility of our own perfection; they can transform the whole of our consciousness. But without our cooperation, they are powerless. Tiger can't change the world, as he said he hopes to do, unless we agree to play along. And if you've come this far, that's what you've done—played a wonderful round with Tiger, and hopefully learned a thing or two along the way.

Perhaps at times I have gone too far in praising Tiger—made him out to be some perfect paragon of virtue. But that is only because I genuinely believe he is a hero for our time. And besides, I'm not the only one gushing. "Tiger blows me away," says the deceptively wise David Feherty, one of Tiger's most vocal fans among those who analyze golf for a living. "People will accuse me of being a brown nose, but I don't care. I know that I am watching something that is truly remarkable, something that I will not get to see again in my lifetime. Years from now we're going to be looking back at this guy and we're just going to think, 'Wow.'"

And yet to me this book is less a tribute to Tiger Woods, though it certainly is that, than it is a testament to the potential of all who read it. By acknowledging Tiger's virtues we recognize our own; by celebrating his greatness we admit that we can be great, too.

And so, as the sun sets on our lovely round, we must make our leave of him and go off on our own. But what a thing it was to watch him play, to witness shots no one could fathom, to see him go further than anyone dreamed. This day is over but there will be another, and soon will come such a day when we, too, can push past limits and see beyond the horizon. And that day will be a glorious day, indeed.

INDEX